OFFICER DOWN!

A PRACTICAL TACTICAL GUIDE TO SURVIVING INJURY IN THE STREET

Dr. Andrew Dennis
Trauma & Burn Surgeon
Police Officer/SWAT

Kendall Hunt
publishing company

Kendall Hunt
publishing company

www.kendallhunt.com
Send all inquiries to:
4050 Westmark Drive
Dubuque, IA 52004-1840

ISBN 978-1-4652-1331-0

Printed in the United States of America

10 9 8 7 6 5 4 3 2

DEDICATION

To every law enforcement professional who puts his or her life on the line to serve and protect the public for no other reason than what is morally just.

To our loved ones, who support us and share in the risks of the everyday unknown.

CONTENTS

FOREWORD

By Brad Thor, #1 New York Times Bestselling Author of "Black List: A Thriller"

There is no job more dangerous in our nation than that of law enforcement officer. Each and every day our law enforcement officers suit up and head out, knowing that there are countless evil souls ready to visit incredible violence upon them as well as upon the citizens they have sworn to serve and protect.

As respect for law enforcement continues to erode in particular circles, as violent offenders place less value on their own lives and on the lives of the people around them, as the potency of mind-altering substances increases, as challenging economic conditions push offenders into more desperate acts, and as the ever-increasing threat of Mumbai-style, Beslan-style, and other terrorist attacks grow in our country, so does the likelihood that the brave men and women who hold that thin blue line between order and chaos, between civilization and anarchy, will be injured in the line of duty.

If, heaven forbid, that happens, how will you survive? What will you do if no one can come to your rescue?

Your number one job as a law enforcement officer is to return home at the end of your shift alive. If you are injured in the course of your duties, that job is going to become very difficult. And if help is not available and you have not trained properly, that job may become virtually impossible.

The bad guys want you dead. We all know that. And in some cases, real life is providing them with better training than the police are getting. That's why your training has to be better. It has to be more focused and more complete. No matter what happens, ***you are going to go home alive.***

With that said, too many law enforcement officers ignore one of the most important areas of training. You may be one of the best shooters on the range and even one of the most proficient ground-fighting grapplers on the mat, but, without proper training in tactical medicine, you are like a parachutist who couldn't be bothered to pack a reserve. And the Medical Tactics for Law Enforcement training presented in this book is just like that reserve—you won't know how badly you need it until it isn't there for you.

Training in tactical medicine cannot only end up making a difference between life and death for you, but also for your partner, other law enforcement officers, and the citizens you have sworn to serve and protect.

Let me be perfectly clear: As my friend, Lt. Col. Dave Grossman, is so famous for saying, you are society's "sheepdogs." You are our "Delta Force."

When it is bad, when rounds are flying, when you are bleeding and those around you are possibly even bleeding out, the emergency medical technicians aren't coming in to help. You are going to have to do their job—and probably while returning fire.

Getting back to that front sight as quickly as possible and putting rounds on the target will mean the difference between life and death for you and those around you. But you will only be able to do that if you have had the absolute best training, have trained like you fight, and then fight like you have trained.

Simply put, there is no better manual on medical tactics for the law enforcement professional than what you are holding in your hands right now. The passion, experience, and dedication of Dr. Andrew Dennis show through on each and every page. As a law enforcement and special weapons and tactics officer, he knows the risks you face on the street every day because he has faced them himself. He knows how bad it can be. As one of the nation's most experienced board certified trauma surgeons, he also knows what it will take to bring you home alive.

Whether through this manual or his exceptional training programs, Dr. Dennis's driving goal is clear: to improve officer safety. He separates medical fact from fiction and will help ***empower you to survive*** and teach you how to ***train to prevail.***

As Dr. Dennis says so well, "If you are ***NOT DEAD,*** you ***CAN*** impact the survival of yourself and others."

Commit yourself right now to never stepping out onto the streets without your weapon, your wits, and what Dr. Dennis can so masterfully teach you about ***staying alive*** and ***staying in the fight.***

ACKNOWLEDGMENTS

When I look back upon my life in search of those who played a part in molding me as a person, there are many. They include my parents, Robert and Linda, and my grandparents, Abe, Marge, and Sylvia. Each played a significant role in exposing me to the world, to history, to my culture, and to the subtleties of life; they educated, scolded, and supported me. Each showed me how to build, to sacrifice, to feel, and to apply emotion, sympathy, empathy, and passion to all I take on.

When I look to those who have influenced me in one direction or another, there are also many. My exposure to those in public safety began with my friends at the Fair Haven Fire Company in New Jersey, and expanded with my colleagues in law enforcement at the Northern Illinois Police Alarm System and Cook County Sheriff's Office in Chicago, Illinois. Collectively, these individuals taught me how to place the good of others above the wants, needs, and safety of myself. From all of you, I have learned the importance of balance.

I am grateful to my colleagues at the Cook County Trauma Unit in Chicago for furthering my education on a daily basis and for being tolerant of my alternate passions.

Special acknowledgment goes to Paul Ouellette, for none of this would have been possible without his vision of me and of my potential. Through his unique passion, Paul has inspired me to create and has taught me step by step how to communicate and to teach so others may benefit from my knowledge and passions.

I thank my loving wife Melissa and my amazing children Minnie and Ethan, who tolerate my contrasting passions and jobs and who inspire me to push on and to grow on a daily basis.

Medical Tactics would not exist without the labor and love of my colleagues Andrew Hamilton, Riley Cooper, Shawn Howd, and my brother Jonathan Dennis.

Finally, I would also like to thank my editor, Michelle Beuscher, Beuscher Consulting, Inc., in Chicago, for all her dedication and care in helping me to organize and express my thoughts in this book.

Sincerely,
Andrew Dennis

CHAPTER 1

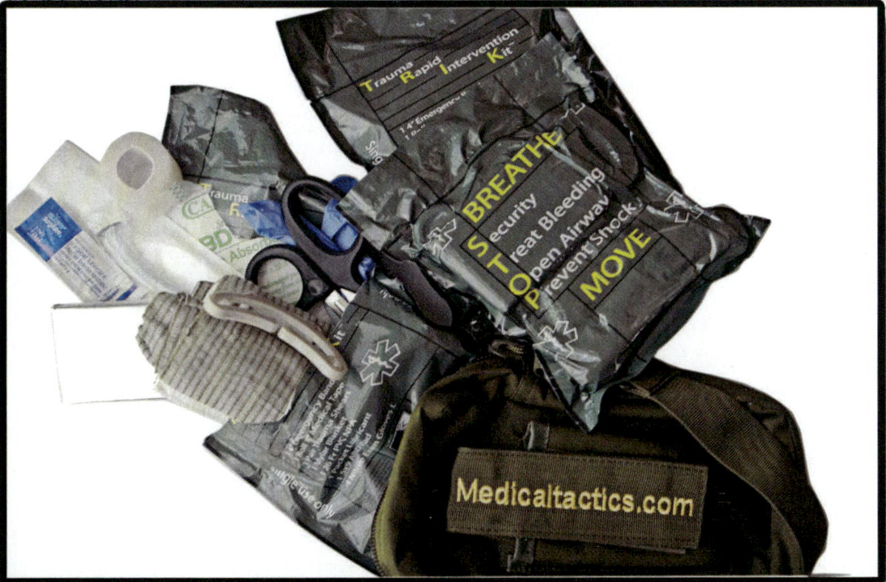

INTRODUCTION

MEDICAL TACTICS FOR LAW ENFORCEMENT AND THE TRAUMA RAPID INTERVENTION KIT, A COMPREHENSIVE TRAUMA RESPONSE SYSTEM

Wearing a police uniform, badge, and gun is like standing on a big red bull's-eye and yelling out "come and get me!" As an officer of the law dedicated to shielding the innocent, you willingly assume the risk as a target for society's menaces.

Odds are at some point in your career that dreaded call "officer down" will ring out. No one wants to address the "the BIG elephant in the room" weighing on the hearts and minds of every man and woman who takes the oath to serve and protect and their families. Thinking or talking about it forces upon us the reality and possibility that the risk of traumatic injury or death exists in a substantial way.

Yet, this elephant is far too big to ignore. You cannot simply stuff down this fear, or run or hide from it. The threat is omnipresent.

Routinely stepping into danger and making life and death decisions come with the territory of enforcing the law and protecting others. It's precisely when police officers are in the most danger that emergency medical services cannot reach them. As a law enforcement officer, you must prepare to be on your own and to take care of your injuries for a minimum of fifteen minutes.

Gunshots, stabbings, battery, vehicular crashes . . . police officers must thoroughly prepare for any imaginable, life-threatening, and worst-case scenario. According to U. S. Department of Justice Federal Bureau of Investigation (FBI) data on *Law Enforcement Officers Killed and Assaulted* in 2011, it is patrol officers who are typically at the greatest risk for felonious assault or death.

According to FBI data collected from law enforcement agencies, nearly 81 percent of 54,774 officers assaulted in 2011 were assigned to vehicle patrols. Among seventy-two law enforcement officers feloniously killed while serving in the line of duty, forty-nine were on assigned vehicle patrol. Officers need the knowledge, training, and tools to effectively treat themselves and, ultimately, to survive and prevail in life-threatening situations encountered whether on patrol or on other field duties.

Serving as a sworn police officer for the past ten years on special weapons and tactics (SWAT) for the Chicago metro area and as a trauma surgeon at Chicago's Cook County Hospital has provided me with a very unique career experience and perspective. I have been a part of law enforcement and emergency medical services for more than twenty years in total. And during this time, I have had the honor and privilege of working alongside and closely observing in action many highly dedicated, amazingly skilled individuals in both fields of law enforcement and medicine.

Through my own personal career experiences and through those of my colleagues in these fields, I have learned a tremendous amount about the job of a law enforcement officer on the front line and through the job of a surgeon in the hospital trauma unit. I have acquired an in-depth, practical understanding of the associated demands, strengths, and liabilities of both roles.

I have seen the results of violence firsthand. I appreciate both the physical and emotional toll it takes on the victims and their loved ones.

Serving in this dual career capacity, I have grown to fully comprehend and appreciate the immense relief that washes over you after a close call. I know what it means for you, your colleagues, and the innocent citizens involved to make it home safe and sound. I have shared in the profound experiences of both success and failure in treating the body and soul of officers injured or killed in the line of duty. I cannot begin to express in words what it means to be able to successfully salvage lives from the brink of death and to send people home with their families as opposed to the unfortunate alternative.

Through this dual experience, I have also had the opportunity to draw some meaningful connections between the roles and glean some unique insights. Whether it's working as an officer out in the street or as a trauma surgeon in the hospital, both roles revolve around the preservation of life.

My personal experiences in the field and my intimate awareness of the statistics on traumatic injuries sustained by law enforcement officers and the associated survival rates revealed to me that current law enforcement education and training is highly deficient where it is most needed. Essential education and hands-on training for addressing *both* the psychological and physical trauma associated with injuries as well as a mechanism for accurately tracking injuries incurred in the line of duty seems to be virtually nonexistent.

Through addressing these deficiencies, I saw a significant life-saving opportunity. Ignoring this "elephant in the room" would otherwise only serve to ignore the value of saving lives. The more the issue weighed on my mind, the more pressing the need for better life-saving education and training for law enforcement appeared to me.

After conferring with my law enforcement and physician colleagues, my perspective was validated, as all individuals I approached concurred with my assessment that there is a serious void in present-day, life-saving education and training for law enforcement. Additionally, using our medical simulation lab, we performed structural assessments of non-medic police officers and the results were consistent and staggering. Without training, few had the tools, mindset, or skills to mitigate injury when it occurred. Moreover, recent U. S. military experience shows that performing simple countermeasures tailored to actual problems and injuries, such as those taught in Tactical Combat Casualty Care training, can potentially make a huge impact toward improving survival on the job (Butler, 2009).

The primary challenges in addressing these deficiencies, however, revolved around narrowing down and clearly defining the problem and then constructing a straightforward methodology for teaching life-saving techniques. The methodology needed to be expressly tailored to the needs of law enforcement. Additionally, it needed to be efficiently delivered in the shortest possible timeframe and in the most effective manner to help preserve educational retention for the long term. In other words, how do we translate technical medical jargon and simplify anatomy and physiology to focus only on the aspects critical to the job of law enforcement while maximizing the individual's long-term retention of the lessons taught?

So began the process of meticulously analyzing the gaps I had observed in existing officer training programs and essential survival tools for field trauma care. Out of this analysis came the development of the Medical Tactics for Law Enforcement (MTLE) training program, on which this book is based, and the accompanying Trauma Rapid Intervention Kit (TRIK).

In 2007, I founded Medical Tactics, a consulting and training company, and led the development of the MTLE training program. I founded Medical Tactics based on the simple, yet critical mission: *Empower to survive, train to prevail.*

Medical Tactics and its team of instructors are dedicated to empowering law enforcement and public safety specialists with essential medical life-saving knowledge, skills training, and tools to respond to traumatic injury and to help improve the survival threshold out on the street. In essence, its purpose is to equip officers both mentally and physically to safely return home to their families at the end of each day.

Much more than your basic first-responder or first-aid class, the MTLE training program is based on a comprehensive trauma response system. A one-of-a-kind, empowering training experience, MTLE seeks to separate medical fact from fiction and to ground decisions in evidence-based logic and psychological strength. MTLE training starts with perception and ends with applied techniques.

In developing the MTLE program, I combined the various real-life experiences and practical insights of a diverse, well-rounded team of professionals from both law enforcement and the trauma unit. This collaborative input has effectively enabled the development of a truly comprehensive, realistic, and useful approach to applying the fundamentals of trauma management and survival.

While other training available in the industry focuses primarily on technical skills development, the MTLE training recognizes that appropriate foundations and perceptions all contribute to mindset, knowledge empowerment, and risk management. All are equally critical in helping to achieve favorable outcomes in dangerous situations. I believe this comprehensive approach to trauma management is what distinctively sets MTLE apart from other training currently available.

Moreover, there is no previous medical training required to participate in the MTLE program. The training is specifically designed for law enforcement and other public safety specialists with the sole purpose of helping them to stay alive and prevail in dangerous situations.

Of course, impossible situations will inevitably arise, traumatic injuries will occur, and lives will be lost in the field. Conversely, there are always opportunities to continuously improve the odds.

MTLE offers a tactical and practical, clinically-based and field-tested approach to survive and prevail in dangerous, life-threatening situations. As of this book's publishing, the one- or two-day intensive workshop has been taught to more than 2,000 police officers, federal agents, and educators with stellar feedback from participants.

Our training and tools are utilized by officers on duty at the local, state, and federal levels throughout the country. The accompanying Trauma Rapid Intervention Kit, or TRIK, has earned the "Member Tested, Member Approved" seal from the National Tactical Officers Association (Whiteley, n.d.).

This book is intended to introduce you to the core elements of the MTLE training system and how the TRIK comes into use relative to providing essential life-saving tools. My hope is that it will make a profound difference for you and for the number of lives we can save together, both on the street and off the street in the trauma unit.

To emphasize what's important to take away from this book, remember, "Preservation of life begins the moment injury strikes. You cannot wait until arrival at the hospital to start applying countermeasures."

What's also important to understand is that reading this book does not replace, or satisfy, the *full* experience to be gained in completing the actual MTLE training program. There is no real substitute for having the opportunity to personally experience simulated field scenarios for applying critical decision-making skills, practical life-saving techniques, and essential tools.

Effective response to traumatic injury is both mental and physical. MTLE therefore teaches the mind and body tactical survival skills to help improve officers' reactions to stress and trauma. The program teaches simple, medically-practiced techniques, covering not just essential training in assessment, bleeding control, airway management, and shock prevention, but it also focuses on the mindset, ballistics as they relate to injury, and rescue assists, drags, and carries.

MTLE was specially designed to integrate the fundamentals of mental preparedness and injury management with the needs of the adult learner. Students take away an overall greater understanding and appreciation for traumatic injury, the necessary tools to help ensure appropriate responses under extreme stress, what is a lethal wound and what is not, when to treat and when not to, and, finally, how to manage such injuries.

Just because an injury looks bad doesn't necessarily mean that it actually is. In an example based on a "Cops" video episode, an officer sustains an ugly laceration on the back of his hand and begins bleeding. Seeing what appears to be a lot of blood, the officer and his colleague begin to panic unnecessarily, drawing their focus away from the scene to the injured hand (20th Century Fox, 2003).

In this scenario, the officer, with his still bleeding and exposed hand, suddenly leaves the scene with his partner in search of the nearest hospital for medical help.

From the officers' diversion of attention to a non-lethal injury and state of mind producing a false sense of urgency and panic, the situation is fraught with pitfalls. There are no large arteries on the back of the hand capable of causing an immediate threat to life. The injured officer himself, or a colleague, could have easily applied direct pressure to stop the low-pressure bleeding of the hand and then carried on with the mission.

This example is not a unique occurrence. Without the benefit of tactical, life-saving knowledge and training, fear-filled emotions naturally dominate the perception of a situation, resulting in poor decision making and flawed actions.

The purpose of the example is not in any way meant to insult officers who have ever reacted in a similar way or assign blame for the situation. Rather, the example is merely intended to demonstrate how easily even experienced individuals can panic and lose control in scenarios involving injuries due to a natural human stress response and lack of appropriate training and education.

> "A little basic knowledge of the anatomy and physiology of human plumbing can go a long way."

Before we investigate this phenomenon further, let's first consider that the number of officers feloniously killed increased considerably from 41 in 2008 to 72 in 2011, according to FBI data. While vehicular accidents were the number one cause of death among police officers accidentally killed in 2011, firearms were associated with the greatest percentage of officers feloniously killed by weapons (Federal Bureau of Investigation, 2011).

FBI data for 2011 further revealed that violent assaults of officers occurred mostly in response to disturbance calls, and officer deaths were mostly associated with arrest situations. Relative to officers slain by firearms, handguns were far and above the most popular weapon of choice for offenders, while the number of shotguns used also increased in 2011 (Federal Bureau of Investigation, 2011).

In virtually any potentially dangerous encounter, both the police and the offender are likely to respond with force. How do you think each party will perform?

Surprisingly, statistics show that offenders are much better shots than officers. When looking at shootings involving officers across multiple information sources, the average successful hit percentage for officers appears to be somewhere between 17 percent and 28 percent. Yet, the average hit percentage for offenders appears to be around 70 percent.

Why is there such a discrepancy? What factors do you think contribute to the unfavorable shooting percentages for officers? The discrepancy can be attributed to a deficiency in the frequency of officer training, being in a defensive and reactionary position, and the natural human response to stress.

On the other hand, 60 percent of offenders have no formal firearms training, while 40 percent have some training (New York Times, 2007; Federal Bureau of Investigation, 1992). Does this surprise you, considering the hit percentage for offenders is generally much higher than for officers?

What factors do you think contribute to this discrepancy in favor of the perpetrator? Logic indicates that being in the offensive position, having trained and been programmed to kill, and possessing a state of mind believing they have little to lose, would be some of the contributors to this discrepancy.

So what are you supposed to do with this information? As a first responder, it is your duty to run toward danger and yet still make it home safely after every encounter.

Simply embracing your natural instincts, based on thousands of years of evolution telling you to turn and run, is not a viable option in the line of duty. You have a mission to survive and prevail, and the people you serve are counting on you to succeed. At the same time, your family and loved ones are all counting on you to return home safely at the end of the day. This is where the Medical Tactics for Law Enforcement (MTLE) training program is critical.

The MTLE development team and training instructors understand the mission, needs, and mental drive required to succeed. When the unexpected occurs and you are faced with injury, you must draw upon a finite set of skills and knowledge to help manage and mitigate injury to survive the encounter and, ultimately, prevail in the situation. We have made it our passion to help empower and train police officers and public safety specialists to provide immediate action trauma care to save oneself or others injured on the street.

To help illustrate, imagine for a moment this classic, worse-case scenario in which you are the first backup officer to arrive on the scene and you spot a fellow officer plus another victim down in clear view but at some distance from your position. Both have been shot and are lying motionless on the ground in plain view. The second victim's identity is unknown. The situation has already been called in over the radio.

How do you respond to this situation? What are your priorities? What are the fundamental considerations? The situation presents a seemingly tough dilemma for which there may be no single right answer, although some options may be more preferable than others.

Most responses fall into one of two major categories: you either choose to go after and eliminate the threat or to focus your efforts on your colleague and attempt to perform a rescue. Both answers may very well be right. Whether you opt to eliminate the threat or perform a rescue, tactics must prevail!

A tactical victory is a must. Both answers pose great risk, and both will ultimately involve a decision tree for medical assessment and care . . . What do you do now? What are your options? Who do you treat first? What, where, when, and how do you apply medical treatment?

So the more important, overall question becomes: *How do you incorporate medical interventions into your tactical variables and vice versa?* As explained, the MTLE training is not just a basic first-responder, first-aid class. Rather, MTLE training teaches you how to marry tactics, mindset, and medicine.

Will your response in the field mirror your response in the classroom? Research shows that officers respond differently in the field than in the classroom.

Recent research led by my colleague Matthew D. Sztajnkrycer, M.D., Ph.D., Department of Emergency Medicine, Mayo Clinic, and published in an FBI Law Enforcement Bulletin revealed that emotions frequently dominate tactics (Sztajnkrycer, Lewinski, and Buhrmaster, 2010). Decisions and actions therefore suffer, resulting in terrible losses. These observations and findings were also replicated in recent MTLE training exercises and soon-to-be-published research from our MTLE development team.

In these MTLE studies, officers were asked how they would respond to a similar scenario. In the classroom setting, almost all of the officers interviewed would eliminate the threat first. In simulated training scenarios performed during our own research, however, an overwhelming majority of the same officers instead performed rescues first. The officers allowed their emotions to influence their decisions and actions at the sacrifice of tactics.

So why do we respond differently in the real-world scenarios? Because of our own worst enemy: *stress.* Perception, fear, mindset, and

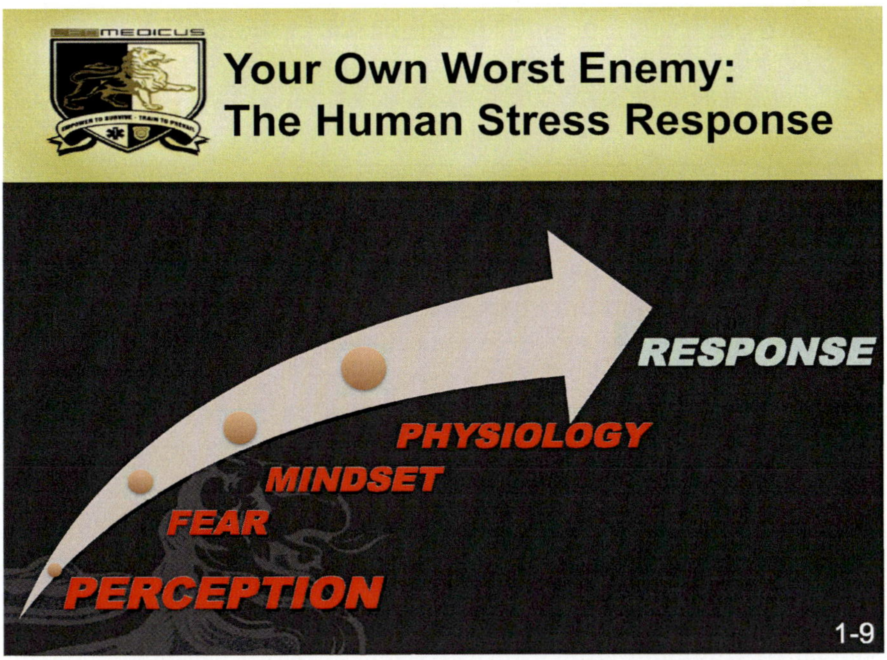

"Your Own Worst Enemy: The Human Stress Response"

physiology all culminate in producing our overall response to a situation and form the basis for our decisions and actions. Our perception of a situation feeds our fear which produces mental and physical effects, and ultimately determines our response. Hence, even the slightest inaccuracy in one's perception can exponentially propagate an overall flawed response under the duress of stress.

The mind and body are integrally connected, and each directly affects the other. In times of extreme stress, both can either work for or against us. To develop an overall understanding of how the mind and body work together in ultimately responding to a situation, it's helpful to dissect the overall process into subcomponents and see how they relate:

- *Perception:* An individual's interpretation and expectation of unfolding events, which are dependent on a conceptual or actual frame of reference.
- *Fear:* An individual's learned response, which is frequently inaccurate or inappropriate and often disproportionate to the actual situation.
- *Mindset:* An individual's psychological preparedness, which responds to the fear.
- *Physiology:* An individual's innate survival countermeasures, including respiration and heart rate, which are designed to maximize the body's physical performance in the face of danger or perceived fear and need to fight or run.
- *Response:* The sequential interplay of perception, fear, mindset, and physiology, which culminates in leading an individual to make a decision and to take action!

So how can you effectively modify and improve your response under stress? Aside from basic human survival instincts, your base of acquired knowledge and life experiences—conscious and unconscious—serve as a frame of reference for determining how you will respond in a given situation. Think of it as a preconceived *script.*

In effect, your mind and body collaborate on the script from which you will act in that situation based on your unique frame of reference. Even if you know something is false, but it's the only bit of knowledge and frame of reference you have to draw upon for that situation, your brain will then treat it as the truth when under stress.

Stories, hearsay, and media and entertainment are all significant sources of input into our scripted responses. Let's put this into the context of traumatic injury and survival. Take, for example, the concept of being shot.

Commonly, one's only frame of reference for what happens if ever shot is what he or she has seen on television or in the movies. Most of the time, the individual on screen quickly dies as a result of a gunshot wound, especially to the torso.

So if Hollywood is one's only frame of reference, then expectations of the event will be based on a dramatized perception rather than actual probability. This, in turn, initiates a cascade of events involving fear-filled emotion that may be unnecessarily amplified. One's ability to cope with this fear and maintain a rational and positive mindset may become impaired.

Subsequently, your body will respond with a genetically programmed, instinctual mechanism to increase oxygen delivery and to blow off carbon dioxide by breathing faster. While this instinctual mechanism serves to enhance performance, it can have a downside if the switch is flipped prematurely or without true cause. At this stage, the cascade of events has progressed to the point where the final decisions and actions may be inappropriate in response to the actual insult or injury.

For example, consider the case of a police officer who was transported from the scene to a nearby hospital after sustaining a gunshot wound to the chest. Despite wearing body armor, the officer patient presented as pale, cold, and clammy with low blood pressure—and was perceived as dying! This was conveyed by emergency medical services en route and confirmed upon arrival in the trauma unit.

Upon closer examination at the hospital, we found no bullet wounds. Rather, the bullet was lodged in the officer's breast pocket notebook. The bullet hadn't even dented the bullet-resistant vest. So if there was no actual injury sustained, how could the officer possibly present as dying?

In this case, the officer perceived the encounter as fatal and went into psychogenic shock. The response was dictated by the officer's conceptual rather than actual frame of reference.

The officer referenced being shot in the chest as a lethal event based on his past experiences, both fictional and real. In turn, he responded with an over-amplified reaction, putting himself into a state of shock.

By definition, "shock" implies that the tissues and cells of the body are deprived of oxygen for some reason or another. Doctors learn the many causes of shock, but few ever see the actual manifestation of all of them during the span of their career.

When most of us think of shock, we generally associate the cause with excessive bleeding, a severe allergic reaction, or overwhelming systemic infection. We often learn of the possibility of "psychogenic" shock in theory, but few ever see it occur in real life. Even fewer see such an extreme case in which an individual's respiratory and cardiovascular system are compromised. In this case, the emotional overload set into play a series of events that culminated in an actual compromise to the officer's physiological functions.

The human body is a wonderful piece of machinery, integrating anatomical structure and physiological function with personality and emotion. As physicians, we actually know very little about this amazing interplay of the physical and metaphysical aspects of a human being. Most of us, however, do recognize our limitations in understanding that there is so much more to learn about the human machine beyond just anatomical structure and physiological plumbing.

So if one's frame of reference can dictate a chain of mental and physical effects culminating in a volatile and catastrophic response, so too shouldn't it be possible to then modify one's frame of reference to produce a predictable and favorable response? In fact, the latter is being done on a daily basis with stress inoculation training methods.

Prime examples of stress inoculation include flight, firearms, medical simulator, live fire and rescue for firefighters, and military basic training. If we can inoculate individuals against stress associated with flying jets, applying cardiopulmonary resuscitation, and performing other high-intensity jobs, then shouldn't we as police officers also be able to preprogram ourselves to more predictably and favorably respond to an injury sustained out in the street?

Fortunately, the answer is a resounding *yes!* We can program ourselves to respond predictably and favorably, provided we have developed a fundamental base of knowledge and been properly trained to apply that knowledge.

The ultimate goal is to script a preprogrammed, predictable, and effective response to as many different contingencies as can be dreamt up. Few will ever acquire the base of actual experiences of responding to the many possible contingencies, so the next best thing is to mimic applying that pre-scripted response by combining a limited, yet highly practical, education of anatomy and physiology with previous experiences, trained skills, and regular practice aids in making better informed decisions for achieving more predictable and favorable outcomes when under pressure.

Law enforcement jobs generally tend to vary a lot on a regional, and urban or rural basis. Law enforcement field jobs also tend to vary widely—from investigations to patrol to SWAT—in terms of risk exposure and intensity.

Additionally, training standards vary vastly across different states and counties, creating the potential for huge variation in experiences and therefore expectations. In essence, perceptions will vary widely.

Tragedy, however, can strike anywhere. Hence, the more standardized a script we can apply, the less variation in perceptions and expectations there will be.

For instance, military service differs from fire service in that military experiences in war time have provided our soldiers with a living library of experiences not seen in peace time. Today's soldiers have a much broader library of experiences to draw upon for dealing with injury. Because they may have seen it before, their perceptions are more accurate. Hence, their subsequent cascade of decisions and actions is less likely to be over-amplified and, in turn, likely to be more appropriate. A similar conclusion can be drawn from the fire service experience, as the variables are probably fewer and training is more standardized.

Remember the commercial airline-pilot hero who miraculously landed US Airways Flight 1549 in the Hudson River? Shortly after taking off from New York's La Guardia airport, Captain Chesley B. Sullenberger III encountered an air collision with birds which caused a double-engine failure (Wald, 2009). Had Sullenberger not spent countless hours training in the flight simulator, could he have possibly been able to successfully land his plane in the river without a single fatality?

Also consider, for instance, what increased our U. S. soldiers' lethality during World War I. Switching from round bulls-eye to human silhouette targets significantly improved soldiers' abilities to successfully hit practice targets. This simple switch to human silhouette targets served to help modify the human psyche and provide a more realistic simulation of hitting an actual target.

Additionally, consider the theory discussed in an article by Brandon Centerwall (1992) in the Journal of the American Medical Association: If it's possible to desensitize a person to violence and lower his killing threshold as a result of playing violent video games, isn't it then conversely also possible to raise one's threshold for survival with video games? This assumption should be true.

As shown with other simulation training programs, it has also been the Medical Tactics for Law Enforcement (MTLE) experience that you can change your frame of reference and ultimately improve your odds for producing a favorable outcome. Appropriate medical interventions practiced under stress can be scripted into a reliable, predictable response.

In effect, you can preprogram, or reprogram, yourself to survive and prevail in the street. Reprogramming requires that you first shed the Hollywood perceptions acquired from watching TV and movies and learn the facts about how weapons cause injury, how resilient your body truly is, and what happens to your body in the event of injury and shock. You can then learn how to condition your mind to better maintain composure and rational thought under extreme stress, apply a basic arsenal of medical countermeasures, and safely move yourself and others out of the danger zone.

This book provides an introduction to the four core elements on which the MTLE training is founded: *mindset, mechanics, management,* and *movement.* Starting with the first element, the chapter on mindset explores how to condition the mind to help limit the negative effects of extreme stress and improve critical decision making in life-threatening situations. The next chapter on mechanics serves to outline the fundamentals of penetrating trauma and separate medical fact from fiction. The management chapter explains how to recognize and when to treat life-threatening injuries. The chapter on movement, the fourth and last of the core elements, explores how to safely and effectively plan and perform assists, drags, and carries to make it out of the hot zone alive.

The book also explains how to use the accompanying Trauma Rapid Intervention Kit (TRIK) which contains all of the tools used in the MTLE training class vacuum sealed into a package small enough to fit into a multitude of locations, including; the cargo pocket of any uniform or duty pants, external tactical vest carrier pocket, or modular, lightweight load-carrying equipment (MOLLE) pouch. To the best of my knowledge, the TRIK is the most comprehensive, compact personal trauma kit available today.

The TRIK is not so revolutionary in its contents. Rather, I see its real innovation more in its "keep it simple" design and practical application to various key trauma care concepts. Not your basic "blue box" first aid kit, the TRIK serves as a "quick-response medical arsenal" specifically geared to empowering individuals with tactical life-saving solutions. The vacuum-sealed kit is also weatherproof and tamper-proof. It even floats!

The TRIK was designed to include the most essential tools of basic trauma care which I believe—based on my own personal experience and on insights gleaned from my colleagues—can make all the difference between survival and death. The TRIK was expressly designed to help any "non-medically trained" individual on the street address both the most fundamental and critical trauma care needs. The TRIK has been adopted by multiple local, federal, and state law enforcement agencies.

The *first* and *most important lesson* you will learn through reading this book and participating in the actual MTLE training program, and learning how to employ the life-saving tools of the TRIK, is:

> You can do this! If you are *not dead,* then you still have a chance and *can* positively impact the survival of yourself and others.

If you are still breathing, you are still *alive!* Sounds incredibly simple, but it can be difficult to remember under extreme stress in a real-life, death-defying situation. The odds of survival are on your side! *You are still in the fight!*

CHAPTER 2

MINDSET

MENTAL CONDITIONING; A MATTER OF LIFE AND DEATH

I firmly believe that surviving life-threatening injury begins with psychological preparedness, which is why I have dedicated an entire chapter of this book to the importance of *mental conditioning.* In this chapter, I will fully explain the rationale for my premise: *your survival on the street comes down to your mind's ability to prevail over the matter of your circumstances.*

Consider that most of your day as a police officer is not spent struggling or engaged in physical violence. Rather, your day is mainly consumed with engaging your mental capacity to communicate clearly and effectively.

In effect, you primarily serve as a subject matter expert on defusing and deescalating situations, using your communication skills and occasionally allowing chaos to work to your advantage. Meanwhile, the risk of becoming involved in a violent encounter persists, always lurking in the shadows waiting for that opportune moment to pounce.

In his book *On Combat: The Psychology and Physiology of Deadly Conflict in War and Peace,* my colleague Lt. Col. Dave Grossman, a foremost expert in the field of human aggression and the roots of violence and violent crime, recounts a Vietnam veteran who segments people of the world among three general classifications: as the flock of "sheep" who make up the population of innocent citizens at large; *YOU* the "sheepdogs," the good guys who serve to protect the flock of innocent citizens from harm; and the "wolves," the bad guys who mercilessly threaten to prey upon the flock (Grossman and Christensen, 2008).

Grossman's analogy is brilliantly simple, and one that I find clearly and effectively resonates with police officers who have participated in the Medical Tactics for Law Enforcement (MTLE) training program. Because you carry a badge and gun and are what stands between the wolves and flock, you are a target—the big, bad wolves of our society will intend to do you harm which you must never forget.

So, if and when you encounter the big, bad wolf, you must be ready. As a sheepdog, you must prepare *both* mentally and physically to safeguard your flock and yourself from hungry predators.

To help limit the negative effects of extreme stress on your body and improve critical decision making in the fight for your life, you must develop a "warrior" way of thinking. The book *Warrior Mindset,* written by Dr. Michael Asken and Lt. Col. Dave Grossman with Loren Christensen (2010), emphasizes the need to develop "Mental Toughness Skills for a Nation's Peacekeepers."

Like the authors, I too have concluded, based on my own personal knowledge and experience gained in the field, that developing mental toughness is absolutely key to one's survival. Developing mental toughness serves to help optimize human performance and improve safety to prevail under pressure.

As illustration, consider the North Hollywood shootout which occurred in the parking lot outside of a bank in February 1997 (History Channel, 2005). Four initial police officers called to the scene sustained various injuries. What's important to note in the example is the *mindset* that each officer chooses to adopt and how he manages the injury.

- *The first, Officer "A,"* sustains a thigh wound and shrapnel wound to the left chest which are *not* instantly life threatening. Officer A's action and mindset: He pulls himself to cover behind a tree—an appropriate, proactive action. From that point on, however, the officer loses his will, taking no further actions of preservation. He essentially resigns himself to whatever may come, be it assistance or death.
- *The second, Officer "B,"* sustains a thigh wound with minimal to moderate bleeding. Officer B's action and mindset: He takes cover behind a parked car and uses his gun belt as a means of compression. The belt compression is actually *not* an effective tourniquet, nor is it very good in controlling bleeding. His actions, however, still declare a proactive mindset to survive.
- *The third, Officer "C,"* sustains a large laceration to the back and flank area, between the hip and ribs, with penetration and moderate bleeding from the wound. Officer C's action and mindset: He runs for cover in an office where a dentist helps to apply pressure to the wound. His actions also declare a proactive mindset for survival.
- *The fourth, Officer "D,"* receives a shrapnel injury to his right ankle. Officer D's action and mindset: He maintains a tactical mindset and receives aid from the dentist who left the shrapnel in the officer's ankle and simply packed the wound—a smart move, as removing the shrapnel at the scene could worsen both the pain and bleeding.

As demonstrated by the four officers in this infamous experience, your life working as a police officer depends on your preparedness and ability to maintain a tactical mindset when the heat is on and the situation begins to escalate. To help further illustrate, think back for a moment to your first violent encounter, shots fired, or cry for help . . .

Where were you? What were you doing? What went through your head? What were your body's reactions? How long ago was this? Even if it was long ago, it is likely that you still have a vivid recollection of the events.

Now, can you remember what you had for dinner just one week ago? Why is it that you can you more easily recall one event and not the other? Isn't it remarkable how we can recall the details of a first violent encounter call even after weeks, months, or years may have passed, yet most of us would struggle to recall the details of what we had for dinner just a week ago? Why is this so?

Our recollection of past events and experiences is linked to our stress response which serves as a protective mechanism. In effect, the mind creates scripts based on our past experiences. These scripts serve to provide a frame of reference so the mind can effectively draw from those experiences again in the future when encountering similar stressful situations.

What about the human body's physical reaction to stress? Can you predict your body's response? Fortunately, you can! Let's examine what typically happens to the human body when acute stress is applied.

Does your heart rate increase or decrease?

Your heart rate increases as stress increases. The increase in heart rate is designed to deliver more blood and, in turn, more oxygen to the parts of the body exerting the greatest demand.

Is your hearing improved or impaired?

Both. Some sounds are amplified, while others are sacrificed.

Are your dexterity and the fine motor skills of your hands and fingers improved or impaired?

Typically, they are impaired.

For instance, think of a classic horror movie where the terrified girl attempts to escape the zombies. She gets into her car and fumbles around as she frantically searches for the key and tries to insert it into the ignition.

In stressful situations, the hands naturally tend to shake. The muscles that work your fingers are actually in your forearms. No one knows exactly why this occurs. Some theorize that it is a function of overstimulation of the muscles. Others think it may be related to oxygen debt accumulating in the muscles.

Under stress, large amounts of adrenaline are released into the body's bloodstream. Adrenaline serves to constrict minor, or peripheral, vessels, allowing the body to divert more oxygenated blood to major vessels that supply the most critical muscles for aiding one's fight for survival. As the peripheral vessels constrict and more blood flow is diverted to the major vessels and most critical muscles, the other, less critical muscles to one's survival may be, in turn, starved of oxygen.

Is your vision improved or impaired?

Typically, your peripheral vision is sacrificed, while your vision for the mission-critical task becomes more focused. Commonly known as "tunnel vision," this defensive mechanism is designed to limit distractions so you can stay focused on the critical task.

What about your rational thinking ability? Is it improved, impaired, or delayed?

Typically, rational thought is delayed. Remember, the human mind depends on predefined scripts to manage stressful situations. Your practical, real-life experiences—"seen it before, been there and done that"—provide the best frame of reference for helping you to maintain more rational thought under pressure.

As further illustration, let's take a look at some actual numbers referenced in *Into the Kill Zone: A Cop's Eye View of Deadly Force,* by David Klinger (2006). The statistics serve to help quantify the temporary perceptual distortion effects experienced in physiological functioning of the human body when subjected to intense stress. Specifically, typical patterns reported in officer responses to violent, life-threatening encounters show: 85 percent with diminished hearing, 16 percent with intensification of select sounds, 80 percent with tunnel vision, 72 percent with visual clarity or focus, 65 percent with slow-motion time warp sensation, 51 percent with selective memory loss, 22 percent with memory distractions, and 7 percent with temporary paralysis.

Nature empowered us with such instinctive physiological response mechanisms to help us maintain focus and manage through unscripted stressful events. "Sound and memory are sacrificed," for instance, "in favor of heightened awareness of the threat in front of us," as Malcolm Gladwell points out in his book *Blink: The Power of Thinking without Thinking* (2005).

An example of this natural physiological phenomenon is also discussed in Klinger's book, *Into the Kill Zone: A Cop's Eye View of Deadly Force* (2006). The noted example reads: "It was like my ears just shut down when we made entry. Then the guy finally brought up his hands, it was like somebody flipped a switch back on and I could hear again."

Our response mechanisms serve to protect us by limiting incoming information in the face of stress. Preventing information overload facilitates the mind's ability to quickly make logical decisions under pressure. Thus, it's important to understand that too much information actually becomes a liability.

Consider the results of an emergency department cardiac study conducted by the Departments of Medicine and Emergency Medicine at Cook County Hospital in Chicago in 2002 (Reilly, Evans, Schaider, Das, Calvin, Moran, Roberts, and Martinez, 2002). This study, cited in Gladwell's *Blink: The Power of Thinking Without Thinking* (2005), evaluated patients who presented to the emergency department with chest pain in one of two ways.

The first group of patients was evaluated by asking them lots of questions regarding their pain and duration, family history, and lifestyle habits such as smoking. A lot of extraneous information not necessarily relevant to the moment was gathered during the evaluation process and left up to the interpretation of the resident physician.

The second group of patients was evaluated using a streamlined set of scripted questions. Only information limited to the event as it was evolving was gathered and coupled with an electrocardiogram, which records the electrical activity of the heart, and lab findings.

This second study group evaluated with the streamlined set of scripted questions demonstrated quicker times to intervention and, ultimately, improved quality of care. Hence, the study results serve to reaffirm the premise that *less is generally best* when it comes to effectively processing information inputs under stress.

Let's look at top athletes as another example. The same premise of less is best seems to apply to their processing of sensory information inputs. Compared to novices, superior athletes are more capable of activating only those parts of the brain which are relevant to the task at hand, according to research conducted by John Milton, a neuroscientist at the Claremont Colleges in California as noted in *Science News* (Bascom, 2012).

Athletes are often described as entering into a "zone-like" state. They seem to have mastered the ability to acutely focus on the task at hand and the ability to tune out distractions or noise.

As noted in Gladwell (2005), when an athlete enters into the zone and reaches that peak performance level, heart function is also maximized. Although based mostly on limited scientific data, there appears to be an optimal state of arousal that may correlate with heart rate, physical conditioning, and experience.

Generally, it is believed that an individual's fine motor skills will begin deteriorating above 115 beats per minute (bpm), as cited in Michael Asken's book *MindSighting: Mental Toughness Skills for Police Officers in High Stress Situations* (2008). However, some conflicting data has begun to emerge. An article by Kathleen Vonk (2008), notes that as the heart rate increases to between 115 beats per minute (bpm) and 145 bpm in a conditioned human body, it appears that a peak state of arousal may be reached which helps to maximize the body's performance.

The Vonk article cites research on this "Optimal Performance Zone" conducted by Bruce K. Siddle and published in his book *Sharpening the Warrior's Edge* (2005). Note that Siddle's studies conducted on this optimal range were associated with physical exertion, or stress, rather than psychological stress.

At what point does the aroused state go too far? When does it begin to work against you or even become downright dangerous?

As theorized by several in the behavioral field, and per Siddle's research highlighted in the Vonk article, when the heart rate surpasses 145 bpm further deterioration of motor skills for performing complex tasks begins to occur. Above 175 bpm, gross motor skills begin to deteriorate. Significant delays, impairment, and eventually the complete loss of rational thought and cognitive processing can occur. These numbers are relative and will vary depending on the individual, the degree of physical and mental conditioning, and the level of experience.

So what happens when the aroused state goes too far? An individual can approach a state of near hysteria, potentially resulting in limited or complete loss of dominating rational behavior.

Think of an irate couple engaged in a heated dispute. As their arguing intensifies, their heart rates spike and blood pressures begin to boil. They begin tuning each other out, shouting over each other, and even throwing and breaking things. Eliciting any ounce of rational behavior in this extreme aroused state is next to hopeless until the couple can step back from the situation, retreat to their corners, and calm down.

Otherwise, the couple's aroused state could further escalate and become physical, resulting in a case of domestic violence. As a law enforcement officer, your training experience teaches you to separate the couple, both visually and audibly, to deescalate the situation and to allow them to each regain self control.

The potential for producing this type of unhinged response, or "mind-blindness," when in an extreme state of arousal is one reason behind banning high-speed police chases and having supervisors make decisions instead of engaged officers, as explained in Gladwell's *Blink: The Power of Thinking Without Thinking* (2005). In high-speed pursuit, officers can get pushed into a dangerous state of mind in which they cannot find the "off-switch." As the heart rate climbs and sensory perception shuts down, decision making becomes flawed. The irrational decision making may not stop with the chase.

Other examples of incidents between law enforcement and offenders that have escalated with poor outcomes have been widely reported in the media. In these incidents, officers have intensified the use of force in attempting to stop and restrain noncompliant offenders. Arguably, both the officers and offenders in these situations may have entered into the state of mind-blindness in which their stress responses were dominated by instinctive impulses rather than knowledge and reason. When instinct dominates in such a situation, the outcome is rarely good.

Is mind-blindness inevitable when the human body is subjected to extreme stress? Fortunately, the answer is *no! Stress inoculation works!*

Although the human mind and body, by nature, features built-in default settings for responding to unscripted stressful events, we humans still prefer and generally perform our best under pressure when we have scripts or reference files. Unfortunately, we do not always have the benefit of accessing scripts for many stressful events that occur as they are by sheer nature often unpredictable and fraught with uniquely challenging circumstances. Thus, we must preprogram, or reprogram where necessary, our default settings for responding to unpredictable events.

When a script is not available, you can still modify your response under stress and improve control over your actions so as not to default purely to an instinctive response which is often tactically flawed. How? By conditioning the mind and body to reference similar scripts enacted in training and daily exercises. Such conditioning enables you to strike a balance between deliberate and instinctive thinking in producing your response and guiding your actions.

Physical conditioning, especially of the heart and lungs, helps to lower the resting heart rate and blood pressure and improve overall heart strength, oxygen delivery per heartbeat, lung function and gas exchange, and related psychological effects. Remember, that ideal heart rate range between 115 bpm and 145 bpm in which the peak state of arousal is reached and performance is maximized best applies to an individual who is physically fit.

Through physical conditioning, for instance, you can increase the amount of time it takes for the heart to approach that upper limit where physical compromise occurs. And by improving your lung function, you can effectively increase your oxygen reserve during times of extreme stress.

More specifically, you can condition yourself and create a more predictable response to stress through intentionally stressing your mind and body, or "stress inoculation." Examples include using electronic control devices (ECDs), adding negative feedback to training, using Simunition, non-lethal training ammunition, role playing, and full or near-full contact training.

Imagine for a moment if you were in a fight for your life and were struck in the gut or kicked in the groin. If you had never experienced such an event, the surprise and inexperience could take you out of the fight. Or worse, it could even get you killed. At the end of the day, scripting comes down to exposure and experience.

On the other hand, if you had previously experienced taking an actual hit or kick, you would have the knowledge and insight to recognize the limitations and consequences caused by such an action. The same applies to being struck, pepper sprayed, or hit with an ECD. You could then predict the duration and extent of your associated discomfort or pain. Understanding the temporary nature of the event would, in turn, enable you to tough it out and stay in the fight until the situation is brought under control.

Whether you consciously recognize it or not in the heat of the situation, you have a script, or at least part of a script; a file you can reference, to help guide your actions. This is why boot camp and other forms of stress inoculation are so successful.

Another way of developing a more predictable response under pressure is through rehearsal. Take the importance of regularly practicing fire drills at home, as discussed in Gladwell (2005). Many people trapped by fire die each year due to smoke inhalation rather than due to the fire itself. Preparing your family so they don't panic by teaching them to get low to the floor and crawl to the nearest known accessible exit is a prime example of the valuable and critical purpose of scripting.

Without the benefit of a previously rehearsed script, individuals stressed from the intense heat of a blazing fire and unable to breath and see in a smoke-filled room will be deprived of their normal senses. As they, in turn, become consumed with fear and a feeling of helplessness, they may begin to panic, jeopardizing their chances of survival. However, through regular fire drills which mimic the possible circumstances with as much reality as possible and teach the escape route options, individuals may significantly improve their chances of successfully escaping and surviving a fire. This fire drill example serves to demonstrate the concept of learned helplessness, which we will explore a bit further later on in the book.

As evidenced by the previously referenced 2002 study conducted by the departments of Medicine and Emergency Medicine at Cook County Hospital in Chicago of cardiac patients admitted to the emergency department and as commonly seen in taking care of the multisystem-injured trauma patient, critical life-saving decision making generally improves with limited information input. Therefore, life and death decisions should not be complicated with extraneous information when relatively little information is actually required. Rather, the methodology for making such a decision becomes more important as a key determinant, or true game changer, in producing a life or death outcome.

As technology continues to improve, we are continuously offered more and more data points to consider. Deciding which data points are critical and which are not is a continuous and growing challenge. We must trust our training, which is often handed down from more experienced individuals to the less experienced students.

To put it another way, sometimes "an egg is just an egg." Although a computed tomography (CT) scan will confirm that it is just an egg, an experienced, confident practitioner will already know that and decline the CT scan. Returning to basics is proving more beneficial, as CT scans provide a significant amount of radiation, which can lead to an increased chance of cancers in the future (Smith-Bindman, R., et al, 2009).

Algorithmic learning offers a highly effective way for preparing how to approach stressful situations and maintain a rational and tactical mindset. Algorithms serve to provide us with simplified approaches and sets of rules to facilitate problem solving. The benefits of algorithms apply to everyone. Few people are so well stress-inoculated as to not need them.

For that matter, even the most experienced surgeon is at risk for a momentary lapse of judgment. For instance, it is not uncommon for a young resident physician to attend to the bedside of a trauma patient who may have an amputated limb and, due to the blood and gore along with the action of the moment, instinctually direct all his focus to the amputation site. Yet, what about the patient's airway? This would be contrary to every teaching the young physician has received as airway, breathing, and circulation (ABCs) are taught as the priorities of life over limb. In this case, the resident is so focused on the amputated limb that he meanwhile fails to recognize that the patient is starting to turn blue. This type of judgment lapse is not a matter of incompetence on the resident's part. Rather, it is a matter of method and conditioning.

As the supervising, or attending, surgeon managing a complicated trauma patient, I have always taught and still believe that the best place to teach is from the foot of the bed, about five feet back. This affords me the opportunity to see all goings-on, the whole picture, as if I were watching a theatre production. It also allows me the ability to recognize failures and successes in decisions and techniques as well as allowing me the opportunity to launch into action and intervene at any second, if necessary.

This is not to say that my surgery team of nurses and residents are not highly competent and capable, but rather that every ship needs a seasoned captain at the helm. In serving the role of captain, I apply my base of knowledge acquired through years of practical experience, including valuable insights gained through both successes and unfortunate losses, to support the trauma team's mission to save as many lives as possible.

My role as a captain, therefore, is to guide the surgery team in the collaborative application of life-saving scripts in response to unfolding events resulting in traumatic injuries. These scripts are designed to help increase the odds of survival for patients admitted to the trauma unit.

As no two patients are ever the same, neither are the life-saving scripts applied to them. In any case, the ability to call on those scripts and past experiences in applying them provides valuable insights and the opportunity to better predict what will happen as unexpected events unfold. The ability to better predict unfolding events subsequently enables the ability to better plan for contingencies and apply lessons learned to stay on top of the situation.

An experienced attending surgeon is always striving to stay a few steps ahead in an operation. The same essentially holds true for any profession where the potential for chaos lurks around the next corner and a wrong move can spell disaster. In other words, what I am describing is the application of a strategic playbook for surviving the game of life in the event it should intersect with unfortunate happenstance.

When operating under stress, it is simply a natural human physiological response for the mind's focus to narrow to the point of losing sight of the bigger picture and other critical aspects unfolding in the heat of the moment, regardless of one's level of knowledge or experience. Thus, a script serves as a means of rescue from such momentary judgment lapses.

Remember learning cardiopulmonary resuscitation (CPR)? CPR training is a classic example of algorithmic learning. Other examples include: advanced trauma life support (ATLS), advanced cardiac life support (ACLS), and the observe, orient, decide, and act (OODA) loop methods of training.

As a more specific example to help illustrate, the first thing medical residents and paramedics typically learn to do first upon arriving at the scene of a cardiac arrest is this basic algorithm or set of rules: stop, slow down, take a deep breath, and take your own pulse. Following this simplified set of rules helps to slow down their breathing and heart rate, improving oxygen delivery and, ultimately, enabling them to better perform CPR and manage the situation.

Algorithms have even served as early childhood development tools. Remember, when you first learned how to say your ABCs? Of course you do! How old were you? Probably somewhere around the age of two!

Considering that there are twenty-six letters in the English alphabet, isn't it pretty amazing that you managed to learn this long sequence of letters at such an early age and have never forgotten them since? And when you say them today, you still likely remember the classic "alphabet song" you learned as a child—"A-B-C-D-E-F-G . . . W and X, Y and Z! Now I've said my ABCs, tell me what you think of me!"

The alphabet song essentially provided you with a simplified script, breaking up the long list of letters into smaller, more manageable and melodic phrases set to a catchy tempo. You may forget what you had for breakfast, but you will not forget your ABCs.

Similarly, simple mnemonics can also be applied to life-saving algorithms. A small research study headed by Dr. David Matlock of the University of Illinois College of Medicine at Peoria, Illinois, demonstrated that performing chest compressions for CPR to the Bee Gees' catchy song hit "Stayin' Alive" helped the study participants maintain close to the ideal 100 compressions-per-minute rhythm standard set by the American Heart Association. The simple and relative song name "Stayin' Alive" is easy to associate with the CPR life-saving technique, and its lively beat is easy to recall under pressure. Weeks later, a second, follow-up assessment of the study participants showed that they were still able to effectively maintain proper technique and perform chest compressions at a speed within the acceptable range. Moreover, study participants' confidence in their abilities to properly perform CPR increased after the training (Lloyd, 2008).

For the Medical Tactics for Law Enforcement (MTLE) course introduced in this book, we too have applied an algorithmic learning method based on a simple and easy-to-remember, three-step script: *BREATHE, STOP, MOVE.*

The first step is to just BREATHE! This is a trigger to simply slow down, reorient, and focus. The importance of this first step cannot be overemphasized. You simply cannot function without breathing. Your body and mind's performance depend on your ability to properly breathe 24/7.

Dynamic breathing, a form of intentional or focused tactical breathing, offers a mechanism to save your life when you are using oxygen faster than you can breathe it into your lungs. It is how your body begins to correct muscle fatigue by trying to keep your body at a normal pH balance of acidity and alkalinity.

In times of stress or even during rapid, robust exercise activity, your muscles use up available oxygen quickly, causing many of your cells to produce lactic acid. Your body naturally converts acid into carbon dioxide. Remember, your lungs exchange the carbon dioxide in your blood for life-sustaining oxygen. It is the level of carbon dioxide in your blood that triggers breathing, not the level of oxygen, as most think.

As acid concentrations increase in one's blood, this acid is converted into carbon dioxide. These increases in carbon dioxide levels trigger your body to breathe faster so you begin to blow off carbon dioxide faster in exchange for oxygen.

Rapid breathing is accompanied by a rapid heart rate which together essentially serve to maximize your physical and mental performance up to a certain point. Beyond this point, however, if your breathing becomes too rapid and your heart rate too high, a counter or negative effect is produced which impedes your physical and mental performance.

Dynamically breathing, however, helps to curb fear, ease anxiety, and slow down the heart rate, allowing you to maintain some sense of calm and gain better control over your mind and body so you can assess the situation before taking action.

The second step, S-T-O-P, stands for secure the situation, treat bleeding, open airway, and prevent shock. STOP serves to provide a means to quickly and efficiently prioritize and deliver tactical medical care in the street. This step delves into the mechanics and management of tactical field care, which is essentially the "nuts and bolts" of practically applying the various life-saving measures taught in the MTLE training program.

The third and final step MOVE involves a quick self test in which you try moving your body from head to toe and looking about in multiple directions. The test allows you to rapidly identify any injuries and limitations to movement. Determining that you can still move serves to reaffirm the fact that you are *not* dead! You are still in the fight!

The three-step, MTLE training script BREATHE, STOP, MOVE is designed to help provide you with an easy-to-recall, tactical approach to help you survive and prevail in a life-threatening situation. The ultimate goal is to help you maintain control in the situation and extract yourself or the victim you are treating out of the hot zone as quickly and safely as possible. Remember, a moving target is harder to hit and therefore less of a target!

Going back for a moment to the first step, BREATHE, how do you dynamically breathe? At a high level, the dynamic breathing technique we teach in the MTLE training program is essentially a modified form of tactical breathing that involves letting the tongue rest against the roof of the mouth as you inhale through the nose and then forcibly exhaling through puckered or pursed lips.

To explain more fully how dynamic breathing actually works, it's helpful to first understand that it draws largely from what is known in the medical field as the Valsalva maneuver. This maneuver serves as a tool in both diagnosing and treating heart conditions, such as an abnormally rapid heart rhythm and associated chest pain.

So how does the Valsalva maneuver work? It essentially serves to increase intrathoracic pressure, which in layman's terms is the pressure within the chest cavity. This increased pressure in the chest cavity, in turn, increases pressure against the vagus nerve which supplies nerve fibers to the heart. As pressure increases against the vagus nerve, it signals to the heart to slow down its pumping action, thereby reducing the heart rate.

In a highly stressful situation, practicing the dynamic breathing technique as taught in the MTLE training program can serve to slow down a rapid heart rate similarly to the Valsalva maneuver so you can gain your composure, think more clearly, and act more skillfully. The simple act of pursing your lips and forcibly exhaling in dynamic breathing increases what is technically called positive end-expiratory pressure (PEEP).

More simply expressed, PEEP is a method of ventilation, or air exchange between the lungs and the atmosphere, which serves to increase air pressure in the chest cavity at the end of exhalation. Increasing PEEP by forcibly exhaling through pursed lips provides a means for helping to increase back pressure, thereby more easily increasing pressure in the chest cavity as well as against the vagus nerve, which ultimately then signals to the heart to slow down.

In effect, when you perform dynamic breathing, you move the diaphragm muscle located between the chest and abdomen downward as you inhale, which serves to push the belly outward and expand the chest area for better air intake to improve oxygenation of the body's circulatory system. As you exhale, you allow the diaphragm muscle to move back upward to the neutral position, drawing the belly inward and expelling the used air from your lungs.

As you breathe in air and hold your breath, you also bear down through your chest and abdomen as if you were going to perform a bowel movement. Bearing down this way helps to dramatically reduce your heart rate. Then you release the hold and forcibly exhale the air through pursed lips. How does the act of bearing down as you inhale and hold the breath help to lower the heart rate?

The heart has two controls. For the purposes of simplification, think of one as the "gas" and the other as the "brakes." Your stress response, or sympathetic nervous system, steps on the gas and accelerates your heart rate.

Remember the vagus nerve we referenced earlier, which supplies nerve fibers to the heart? By bearing down through your chest and abdomen as you breathe in and hold your breath, you effectively apply pressure to the vagus nerve, which therefore acts as the brakes and thus decelerates the heart rate.

This same braking mechanism is also a factor in why so many people die on Sunday morning reading the paper while moving their bowels on the toilet. So why on earth would you then want to practice this type of dynamic breathing under pressure?

First, it's important to differentiate between a healthy and physically fit person and a person who is not. The people who die while bearing down during a bowel movement typically have moderate to severe heart disease and poorer blood flow. So, when they stimulate the vagus nerve by bearing down, their heart rate and blood flow slows down too much. Because blood flow is already compromised due to their clogged arteries, any further decrease may cause them to pass out or have a heart attack.

On the other hand, in a healthy and physically fit person, bearing down in performing dynamic breathing offers the benefit of slowing down the heart rate to help a person relax and maintain composure under duress. Rather amazing, isn't it, how such a seemingly simple function as taking time to just breathe using this relatively easy-to-perform dynamic breathing technique can serve as such a powerful tool in a law enforcement officer's arsenal to survive and prevail?

Additionally, combining dynamic breathing with movement allows you to break the tunnel vision effect and take inventory of the situation. In effect, maintaining a fresh supply of oxygen to your brain literally preserves your ability to see and think straight so you can either confirm or exclude injury and make your move. A steady oxygen supply is also essential for fueling your organs and muscles so you can quickly move to safety.

While the MTLE training methods are designed to help improve your physiological stress response and increase your chances of survival, it is important to understand that your mental perception of a situation can also largely influence the outcome for better or for worse. Your perception of a situation fuels your fear, which initiates the natural human "fight or flight" response.

Your perception and fear-based response are rooted in anxiety over the unknown. Your negative perception of a situation causes mental stress which, in turn, causes the body to react by dilating the pupils, increasing the heart rate, narrowing the field of vision, and excluding certain sounds. Fortunately, you can actually master such fear by altering your perception. When mastered, you can learn to draw on your fear to help you stay in the fight. In effect, your fear can even serve as a powerful motivator, giving you that edge to overcome potentially insurmountable odds. Fear can serve as a trigger for previously written mind scripts.

First, it's important to understand that fear is a *learned* response. The feeling of helplessness, or lack of control, is learned. For example, children may not begin to grasp the concept of death until around age six or so. Think of a younger child on a downhill ski run.

The young novice skier virtually shoots straight down the mountain, making very few turns with no fear of speed or crashing. He doesn't learn to fear crashing until he takes his first jarring tumble down a run. From that point onward, his perception of the mountain changes and the newly associated fear of crashing leads him to ski down more cautiously and learn to develop better control of his skis.

By altering your perception of a situation, you can, in turn, alter or minimize your fear. This change in perception helps to curb your body's physiological stress response, enabling you to maintain better control of the situation and make more rational decisions. This premise has been well demonstrated in humans, such as in practicing fire drills with children (Seligman, 1992).

The premise has been further supported in research conducted by Dr. Martin Seligman of the University of Pennsylvania (1992). Dr. Seligman states, "Your thinking determines your behavior." As support for his statement, he conducted experiments at the university, placing dogs in the middle of a maze with four different ways of getting out.

Dr. Seligman's research results showed that if a dog was shocked before being shown a way out of the maze, he would just sit down and resign himself to take the shocks, never seeking a way out. On the other hand, if a dog was shown a way out of the maze prior to being shocked, he would run to the exit upon receiving a shock.

So how can you modify your perception and curb your fear of a situation? One way is to lessen the unknown.

What does it feel like to get shot, for instance? People who have been shot and survived have recollected and described various perceptions of the event. Some say that it felt like getting hit with a round of training ammo, while others say it was similar to being stabbed by a hot poker. And others say they never felt it until after they saw blood or the wound.

Fear of the unknown, injury, and death naturally dominates our thinking in life-threatening situations. So if you can condition yourself beforehand through "stress inoculation," or learning and experiencing how it feels to get shot, for instance, then you can modify your perception and lessen the grip that fear has on you. This is why practicing with training ammo in simulated situations is better than simply shooting at paper targets.

Another important lesson learned in MTLE training is the need to *train often* for what you know and *do the least.* Mental exercises, such as imagining worse-case scenarios and playing the "what if" game, can help prepare you to save your life in reality. Charles Darwin (1859) indicated that the most adaptable of the species is more likely to survive than either the strongest or the most intelligent.

Playing the game can help you mentally prepare and rehearse for what you would do in an actual situation. Imagine what you would do, for instance, if your life or the lives of your partner, spouse, or child were at stake.

Train as if you are really in the fight. The human tendency is to get comfortable or complacent with training over time. We tend to spend our time primarily training in things we are already good at and not push ourselves out of our comfort zone. To maintain a sharp edge, however, you must train for what you are least comfortable doing no matter how uncomfortable or hard it is.

MTLE training therefore becomes a way of life which must be constantly reviewed and practiced. Looking for practical applications to apply MTLE training in your everyday life can help you internalize the training so that it becomes a predictable and automatic response under pressure. You owe it to yourself, your partner, and your colleagues to adopt this way of life to help ensure survival in the street. What's more, you also owe it to your family and loved ones, who all count on you to come home at the end of each day!

CHAPTER 3

MECHANICS

FUNDAMENTALS OF PENETRATING TRAUMA AND MEDICAL FACT VERSUS FICTION

Because law enforcement officers undergo training to carry and use a firearm, it's a natural assumption that they are all experts in firearms. However, this assumption is much overstated and more often than not is inaccurate.

Based on years of practical knowledge and experience acquired by working in the field, it is my firm belief that the basic officer firearms' training does not an expert make. While most law enforcement officers are familiar with their own weapons, few have in-depth knowledge of firearms and edged weapons overall, and the types of bodily injury they may cause.

Wound ballistics is the study of the effects of penetrating projectiles on the body. Because there are so many variables to consider, wound ballistics tends to be a somewhat inexact science and, therefore, a challenging study.

Contrary to common theory and media reporting, law enforcement officers are trained to "shoot to stop"—*not* shoot to kill, *not* shoot to disarm, *not* shoot to wound. For those of us who actually train with a firearm, we understand that the accuracy rate of striking a target with a handgun is generally relatively poor. Moreover, the success of accurately striking the target decreases significantly when we add stressful distractions to a firearm situation (Hurley, 2006).

Depending on what source you read, averages cited for successful hits in actual shootings generally range somewhere between 17 percent and 28 percent (Hurley, 2006; Kelly, Raymond, Farrell, and Gerrish, 2007). Hence, it is unthinkable and unreasonable to assume that an officer in fear of his or her life could successfully manipulate a bullet to only disarm, maim, or surgically incapacitate an offender. It just doesn't happen, and it is foolish to think it can reliably occur. This is *not* Hollywood; this is real!

At the end of the day, ballistics, wounding, and ultimately hitting or stopping, an offender comes down to many different variables. The size, shape, velocity, and construction of the projectile play only a part in the effectiveness of the strike. Injury and survivability also depend on the tissues and organs involved and their tolerance to injury, as well as both the psychological and physiological make-up of the individual struck.

Although most individuals associate the caliber of a weapon with its ability to inflict injury, it is a rather inaccurate assumption. It is much more than a matter of caliber. Rather, it is the culmination of multiple variables at play.

Again, we see that an inaccurate perception can negatively affect one's decisions, reactions and actions. For example, many associate a strike with a 45-caliber missile as much more lethal than a strike by a

9-millimeter round. In fact, this is a very inaccurate perception and can lead to an unjustified fear, a predetermined negative mindset, and possibly a physical and psychological response that is in error. Let's take a look at these different variables and how they may impact our understanding and decisions in a situation.

Wound severity is only partially dependent upon available kinetic energy and physical characteristics of the projectile, or bullet, discharged. Other variables include physical characteristics of the targeted body part, behavior of the bullet in the relative body part tissue, and clinical consequences of the tissue injured. While each of these variables plays a significant role in wounding, the three most important are *kinetic energy* and the *density and elasticity qualities of the tissue struck*. Survival, in turn, is frequently influenced by the tolerance for injury of the part of the body that is struck.

Kinetic energy, the energy of motion, is determined using the mass and velocity of the elements involved. So, relative to an officer discharging a firearm, energy of motion fundamentally means the work required to accelerate an object, the bullet in this case, from a state of rest to a state of action, or movement, from one place to another. In other words, the work it takes to transfer the bullet from the muzzle of the officer's firearm into the targeted body part of the offender.

Relative to kinetic energy, the mass represents the weight of an object, or the bullet. Velocity represents the speed of the bullet.

In categorizing different types of firearms, they are generally divided into low, medium, and high velocity. Keep in mind that these categories have variable definitions, but we will define them for our purpose as follows: low velocity firearms (less than 1,100 feet per second) include handguns with the exception of Magnums; medium velocity firearms (between 1,100 and 2,000 feet per second) include shotguns and Magnums; and high velocity firearms (greater than 2,000 feet per second) include rifles.

While velocity is important, it is not the whole picture. Consider, for instance, that a 9-millimeter handgun round flies at approximately 1,100 feet per second and creates approximately 416 foot pounds of force. A 45-caliber round flies at approximately 800 feet per second and creates approximately 350 foot pounds of force. Both can create similar or dissimilar wounds, depending on the tissue struck.

A knife, however, is a very low-velocity weapon. And yet, a knife can still cause an awful lot of damage and often proves fatal.

In effect, velocity is only a small part in determining the extent of a wound. Rather, it is much more about the energy "dump," or transfer, from the muzzle of the weapon, to the flying bullet, and ultimately into the intended target. What do we mean by energy transfer?

To help understand the concept of energy transfer, it's helpful to visualize a scenario in which an officer shoots his gun at an offender. When the gun discharges, the bullet leaves the muzzle with potential energy. As the bullet strikes the targeted body part, the potential energy becomes kinetic energy. This kinetic energy is then transferred into the target.

In effect, the transfer of kinetic energy into the target is what determines the nature of the wound. How much energy is transferred into the target depends on a number of variables, including: kinetic properties of the bullet, such as the elements of mass and velocity used in determining kinetic energy; morphologic properties of the bullet which pertain to the shape, construction, and flight characteristics; target body tissue density and elasticity qualities, and essential value to survival, such as the liver versus a lung or a large versus a small blood vessel; and length of the wound tract.

Keep in mind, the better a tissue is at absorbing this energy, the more tolerant the tissue will be to the injury and typically the less severe the injury. For example, the lung is less dense and more elastic than the liver or bone. It can stretch and better accommodate the cavitation caused by the energy transfer. It will thus be better able to preserve its blood supply and therefore limit the degree of injury.

How much damage can a bullet from a discharged firearm cause? First, it's helpful to understand that bullets of equal wounding potential can produce very different wounds, depending on factors other than mass and velocity.

Remember, kinetic energy plays a big role in wounding. To simplify, let's break down the elements of the formula for determining kinetic energy (KE): kinetic energy = ½ mass × velocity squared, or more formulaically written: $KE = \frac{1}{2}MV^2$. Because velocity is squared, smaller changes in velocity will result in greater changes in kinetic energy.

The formula for kinetic energy reduces the mass figure by dividing it in half. On the other hand, the velocity figure increases as it is squared, or multiplied by itself.

Remember, we stated earlier that wounding is determined by the interplay of multiple variables with the two most important being kinetic energy and the density and elasticity qualities of the tissue struck. Now that we have addressed kinetic energy, let's take a closer look at other key variables, such as tissue tolerances which are based upon both *density* and *elasticity* of the target tissue.

First, what happens when energy is transferred into the target tissue? Energy can neither be created nor destroyed; it must be transferred. In the case of a bullet striking tissue, the energy is transferred to the tissue as the bullet slows down within the tissue. The more resistance the bullet encounters, the quicker it is slowed and the more rapidly the energy is transferred.

Additionally, energy can be transferred to the missile itself if it were to deform and fragment. Both of these actions require energy. When energy is transferred to a tissue, it can be absorbed with either little destruction or significant destruction. Less destruction tends to occur with less dense tissues that are more elastic and forgiving, like the lung. More significant destruction tends to occur with more dense tissues that are less elastic and unforgiving, like the liver and bone.

Regardless of its size, when a bullet breaks apart, it loses energy faster. The energy is effectively transferred to the bullet to break it up, and then transferred from the bullet into the targeted tissue. Striking some dense body tissues may cause the bullet, as well as the tissue, to break up. Striking a bone is a perfect example of this action.

As a bullet fragments upon entering body tissue, each piece becomes slower and less aerodynamic and fluid dynamic, thus encountering more resistance. In effect, each piece has less energy than the whole. And each piece will continue to lose energy.

But how exactly is energy transferred from a bullet as it penetrates body tissue? For our purposes, energy may be transferred three different ways: permanent cavity, temporary cavity, and sonic pressure wave.

The transfer of energy into target tissue through the formation of permanent and temporary cavities is also referred to as "cavitation." Crushing and ballooning are the principle mechanisms by which bullets impart damage to body tissue.

Energy is also transferred via the sonic pressure wave carried with each flying bullet. For reference, consider that the speed of sound travels at 343.2 meters per second (1,126 feet per second). Many handgun bullets fly close to the speed of sound. For example, a bullet discharged from a .45 Automatic Pistol travels at approximately 800 feet per second. However, a bullet discharged from a 9-millimeter Luger travels at approximately 1,100 feet per second!

Now that we have established an overall understanding of how energy is transferred, let's take a closer look at the two different types of cavitation created as a bullet penetrates body tissue: *temporary* and *permanent.* The creation of a temporary cavity is the transient or short-lived ballooning of the wound tract, as the tissue will ultimately collapse back. On the other hand, a permanent cavity is created as tissue is crushed. The tubular wound tract of crushed tissue directly relates to the size and shape of the actual bullet: it is the hollow tube within the target tissue that is left after the bullet passes through. For those who remember their high school physics, fluids behave differently than solids; they are non-compressible.

So what happens to a fluid-filled container when it is struck by a bullet? What is the effect of cavitation on the closed, fluid-filled container? Have you ever shot at a jug full of water at the shooting range? What happened when the bullet struck the filled jug? Most likely, it exploded.

What happens if you shoot an empty jug? The bullet goes right through the container, in and out, and then simply falls over. Why?

Why does the effect of cavitation in a fluid-filled container differ from body tissue with a couple of exceptions? The reason is that fluid is non-compressible, resulting in an explosive-looking failure of the container. When it is displaced fluid moves as a single mass. As the fluid seeks to move along the path of least resistance, the only place it can go, in this case, is out the path, or hole, created by the bullet.

Relative to body tissue, there are a couple of areas of the body that mimic the effect of cavitation in a fluid-filled container. What are they? What structures in a body are essentially closed fluid-filled vessels? If you guessed the heart and bladder, you are correct. Interestingly, each behaves quite differently. Why and how so? Keep these exceptions in mind, as we will come back to body tissues and their strategic importance.

As a bullet penetrates a human target, it decelerates and "dumps" its energy into the body tissue, therefore creating the largest cavity in the area where the most energy is dumped. The greater the retardation, the greater the impact and energy transfer—and the bigger the cavity.

To help further illustrate this concept, let's take a look at an example of a police officer involved in a shooting. The officer used a Colt AR-15 .223 caliber semiautomatic rifle to shoot a sword-wielding individual. The discharged bullet struck the offender in the left upper quadrant of the abdomen, striking a rib. Upon striking the very dense rib, the bullet subsequently lost most of its energy right away and, as a result, produced a large cavity in the left upper chest and abdomen. The left side of the diaphragm muscle as well as the spleen and kidney were blown apart. The injuries were unsurvivable due to the rapid and large volume of blood loss.

We have examined at length the three foremost variables in determining wounding: kinetic energy, and density and elasticity qualities of tissue struck. But what other variables also come into play? *Bullet de-*

sign is another important variable that warrants consideration. Therefore, it's helpful to compare the design of handgun versus rifle bullets.

Handgun bullets are relatively larger in caliber, short and squat, round-nosed, jacketed or partially jacketed, with a low-to-moderate kinetic energy measuring between approximately 300 and 500 joules of energy. In contrast, rifle bullets are more often smaller in caliber, long, thin and unbalanced, with a much higher kinetic energy ranging between approximately 2,000 and 3,000 joules. Keep in mind that the kinetic energy is based mostly on velocity.

As an example, musket balls, usually made of lead, will deform and thus increase the diameter of the wound tract and crushed tissue. Additionally, by rapidly deforming, they lose their tissue dynamics and therefore cause a more rapid deceleration and, thus, large cavitation and tissue destruction. When combined with high velocity, such wounds can prove devastating.

Rifle bullets pose a unique issue. Typically flying at a very high velocity and thus possessing significant kinetic energy, they hold the potential to inflict massive tissue damage. Calibers of center-fire rifle bullets such as a .223 or .308 are similar to handgun ammunition in weight, but their wounding potential is greatly enhanced by the velocity of the round.

With high velocities of greater than 2,000 feet per second, a temporary cavity is formed along the wound tract. The temporary cavity may increase, for instance, up to twelve times the diameter of the bullet or more. Temporary cavitation in combination with direct tissue disruption and energy transfer from the bullet through fragmenting and tumbling may contribute to the size of the injury.

Caliber, an old nomenclature system of measuring ammunition using the internal diameter of a firearm barrel or bore, or the bullet, is not a useful indicator of wounding potential on its own. Decimals of an inch are also commonly used for measurement purposes. The more modern system of measurement used today is millimeters. For example, the .38 Smith & Wesson Special, .357 Magnum, and 9-millimeter handgun rounds are all essentially the same in diameter. However, the .357 Magnum's longer cartridge case holds more gun powder, increasing the velocity and kinetic energy of the discharged round. As another example, a .223 caliber rifle round is a similar diameter to a 22-caliber handgun round. However, the relative velocity and kinetic energy is much higher for a .223 rifle round, hence it has greater wounding potential.

Regardless, missile size plays only a limited role in wounding. Interestingly, it seems to play a more psychological role than a physical role.

The bottom line: While caliber is somewhat of a variable to consider, it carries a relatively less significant weight in determining the wounding potential or lethality of a firearm. Kinetic energy and target tissue characteristics are still the primary determinants.

Relative to wounding and ballistics variables, there are still some other aspects of bullet design worth considering. For instance, consider the difference between a hollow point and a full metal jacket round, which provides a premise for great debate about the science of ballistics. Is a hollow point round more lethal than a full-jacketed round?

A hollow point round has only a partial or no metal jacket. Thus, it is intended to deform and flatten out in shape like a "mushroom" upon target impact. The shape change, in turn, increases the retardation, or stopping power, and the kinetic energy transfer of the round into the body.

Because a hollow point round is designed to limit over-penetration, it has the potential to penetrate less deeply into body tissue due to the early energy transfer design. It may not reach protected organs, major vessels, and nervous system pathways located deeper within the body. Again, this is dependent upon multiple "ifs" or other variables.

The hollow point round mushrooms in shape upon impact; it increases the diameter of the permanent wound cavity, potentially by as much as two-and-a-half times. Moreover, the overall wound tract, including the temporary cavity, may increase several fold as well.

Why do law enforcement officers commonly carry hollow point ammunition? Because the hollow point round is designed to transfer most of its energy early on upon impact, and the risk of over-penetration into both the intended and unintended targets is reduced. In effect, the hollow point is intended to come to a quicker stop.

Conversely, a full metal jacket round is designed to produce minimal shape change upon target impact. As a result, retardation is minimized. A full metal jacket round therefore has the theoretical potential to penetrate more deeply into the body, while the energy transfer upon impact is lessened. The result is reduced cavitation and wounding. However, if the full metal jacket round can reach deeper to strike protected, higher-value tissues, such as large blood vessels and neural pathways, then potentially it can be argued to be more lethal.

In the end, the debate rages on due to the fact that bullets cause injury, and death continues to plague society.

Consider, for instance, that when a round strikes more dense body tissue, its shape naturally deforms, reducing the risk of clinical consequence. Whereas when a round strikes softer, more compliant and

Bullets, non-deformed and deformed, image.

elastic tissue, such as the stomach, a larger amount of energy may be absorbed with less clinical compromise.

In one such case, a bullet was shown to have penetrated the abdominal wall, ultimately coming to rest inside the victim's stomach. In order for the bullet to stop where it did in the stomach, it must have dumped all of its energy into the tissue.

Because it was a hollow point missile and showed no evidence of deformation, we know it struck only soft, absorbent tissues which were able to stretch and accommodate all of the energy transferred. Since the stomach and surrounding tissues showed little actual injury, this hypothesis was confirmed. Hence, all the energy was transferred into the stomach rather than the bullet itself.

A perfect analogy would be an aircraft landing on an aircraft carrier assisted by an arresting net. The compliance and stretch of the net are able to accommodate the massive amount of energy transfer needed to bring the plane to a stop.

Let's take a look at yet another variable known as yaw, or the deviation of the longitudinal axis of the bullet from its original line of flight as it leaves the barrel. In simple terms, the bullet twirls, or turns, as it flies through the air. Yaw increases to its maximum value early in flight and decreases later in flight.

As a bullet yaws, it basically tumbles into the target, increasing energy transfer into the body and contributing to increased cavitation and a larger wound. Thus, the greater the tissue density, retardation, yaw, and energy transfer, the greater the overall combined effect for producing more severe tissue injury.

With an understanding of the variables discussed thus far, which type of handgun would you prefer to carry to defend yourself? And why?

When it comes to wounding and lethality, it's important to recognize that the difference in handgun rounds is actually fairly minimal. Rather, the best answer is based on the understanding that accuracy is the biggest hurdle to overcome. So your preference should be for the handgun that offers you the greatest shooting accuracy.

What about shotguns? The shotgun is designed to fire multiple types of pellets: a soft shot made of lead, hard shot made of alloy, plated or jacketed shot, and steel shot. Shotgun pellets are classified into two general categories as either *buckshot* or *birdshot.* The greater the shot number, the smaller the diameter of the pellets.

Typically a much larger size of shot, the buckshot includes pellets measuring greater than 0.14 decimals of an inch in diameter, allowing for less than 100 pellets per shell. A comparably much smaller size of shot, the birdshot includes pellets measuring less than 0.14 decimals of an inch. A birdshot allows between 200 and 300 pellets per shell.

The caliber of a shotgun is defined by the term "gauge," which essentially refers to the number of lead balls of a given bore diameter making up a pound. For example, a 12-gauge shotgun equates to 12 lead balls making up a pound.

Shotgun slugs can weigh up to 200 times greater than handgun ammunition. They can cause massive damage. The kinetic energy associated with a shotgun round is very high given that the velocity usually approaches somewhere between 1,300 and 1,500 feet per second. For example, take "00" buckshot consisting of a quantity of eight to nine nearly 9-millimeter pellets. That is the equivalent of nine 9-millimeter rounds all firing at the same time in close proximity and at velocities greater than 1,300 feet per second. Thus, the buckshot is generally very effective in hitting its target and causing massive tissue destruction.

The "mass" of shot, or collection of pellets, discharged together as it leaves the barrel is what makes shotguns unique. From there, each individual pellet carries with it the potential for creating a permanent cavity and a temporary cavity. Moreover, the entire mass of shot carries with it the potential for creating a permanent cavity and a temporary cavity. The overall size of the cavities produced ultimately will be determined by the proximity of the target to the gun barrel, as the shot separates as distance increases. Hence, at close range, the shot flies together. But as the distance increases, the shot begins to spread out.

Taking a closer look, the basic composition of shotgun ammunition includes a plastic case, the shot or slug, a paper wad or plastic cup, powder charge, brass head, and primer. Every shotgun shell is packed in a plastic case with a brass head. Between the powder charge and the shot is a paper wad or plastic cup. Typically, the wad or cup flies from the barrel together with the shot, but falls off quickly as it opens up like a sail. The shot, however, continues on toward the target in a tight group. As distance to the target increases, the wad or cup encounters more resistance and begins to slow quickly. The shot continues to fly forward ahead of the decelerating wad or cup.

Depending on the manufacturer, the distance at which the wad or cup falls off and the shot begins to spread will vary. Typically, at a closer range of about seven yards or less, both the shot and the wad or cup will strike the target but not in the same spot. This has potential clinical significance, especially for the surgeon, as the plastic cup or paper wad may not show up on an x-ray. Thus, the surgeon needs to keep in mind the possibility that either could still be lodged in the wound and may even be left there if the surgeon does not actively pursue them.

Projectiles, both lead and metal alloy, may be left within the body and pose little, if any, clinical relevance to one's recovery. An exception is a lead bullet lodged within a joint. The lead from the bullet can be chelated by the synovial, or lubricating, fluid of the joint and subsequently leach out into the bloodstream, resulting in a harmful, elevated blood level of lead. In fact, the most common question we are asked at the Cook County Trauma Unit is also the slogan on our shirts: "Did you get the bullet out?" Surprising to most who ask is our answer of "no."

Now, let's evaluate wounds caused by shotguns. Consider this case in which an individual is hit by a shotgun at close range. We see that his liver is protruding through a chest wall defect measuring approximately two inches in diameter. Do you think this individual survived? As bad as it sounds, surprisingly, he did survive the injury.

How is this possible? In his case, most of the kinetic energy was absorbed by his chest wall and ribs prior to striking the liver, hence the large wound site caused by the cavitation. The damage continued into

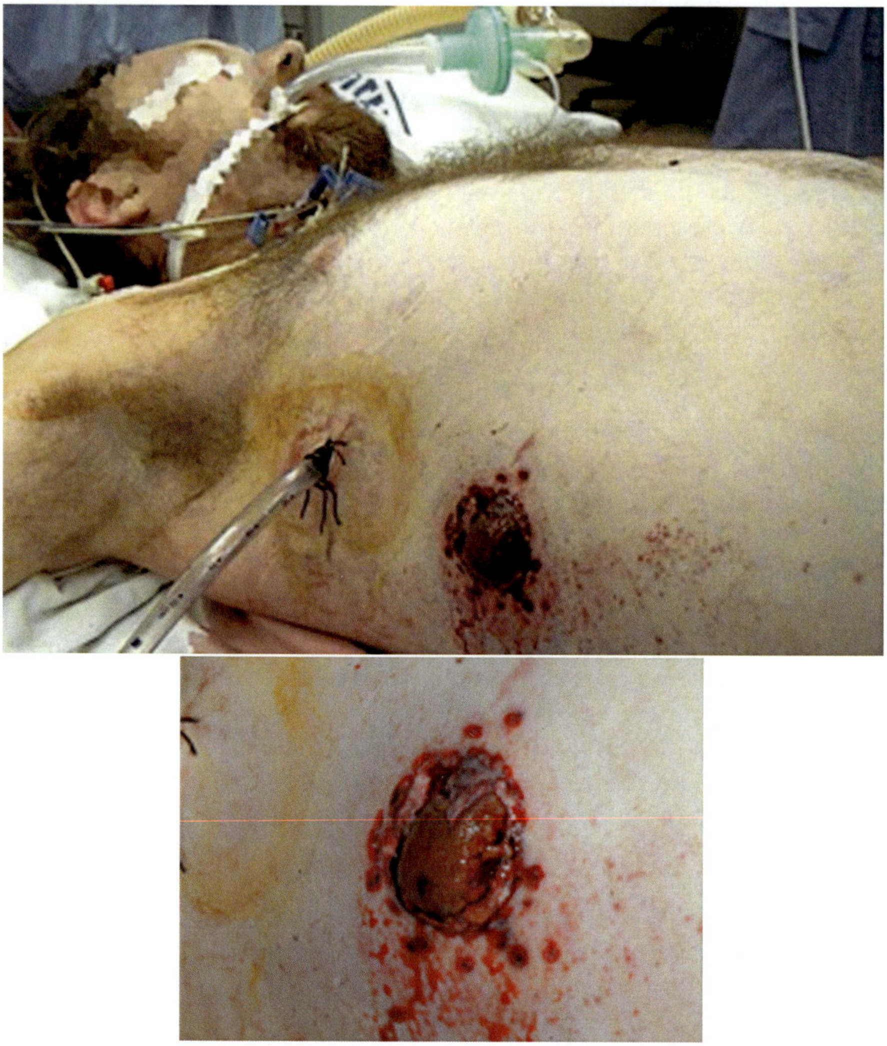

Shotgun wound to chest and liver.

Iwanicki, Michael, D.O., Director of Trauma Services, Co-Director of Critical Care Services, Advocate Good Samaritan Hospital, Downers Grove, Illinois.

the liver and diaphragm. However, due to the small caliber of the shot, the location of his diaphragm when the strike occurred and the fact that most of the kinetic energy was transferred to the chest wall and lungs, sparing the liver, he fared well in the end.

Initially, the individual's biggest problem was excessive bleeding. After he was stabilized and had survived the bleeding risk, addressing his next biggest problem involved the reconstruction of his chest wall.

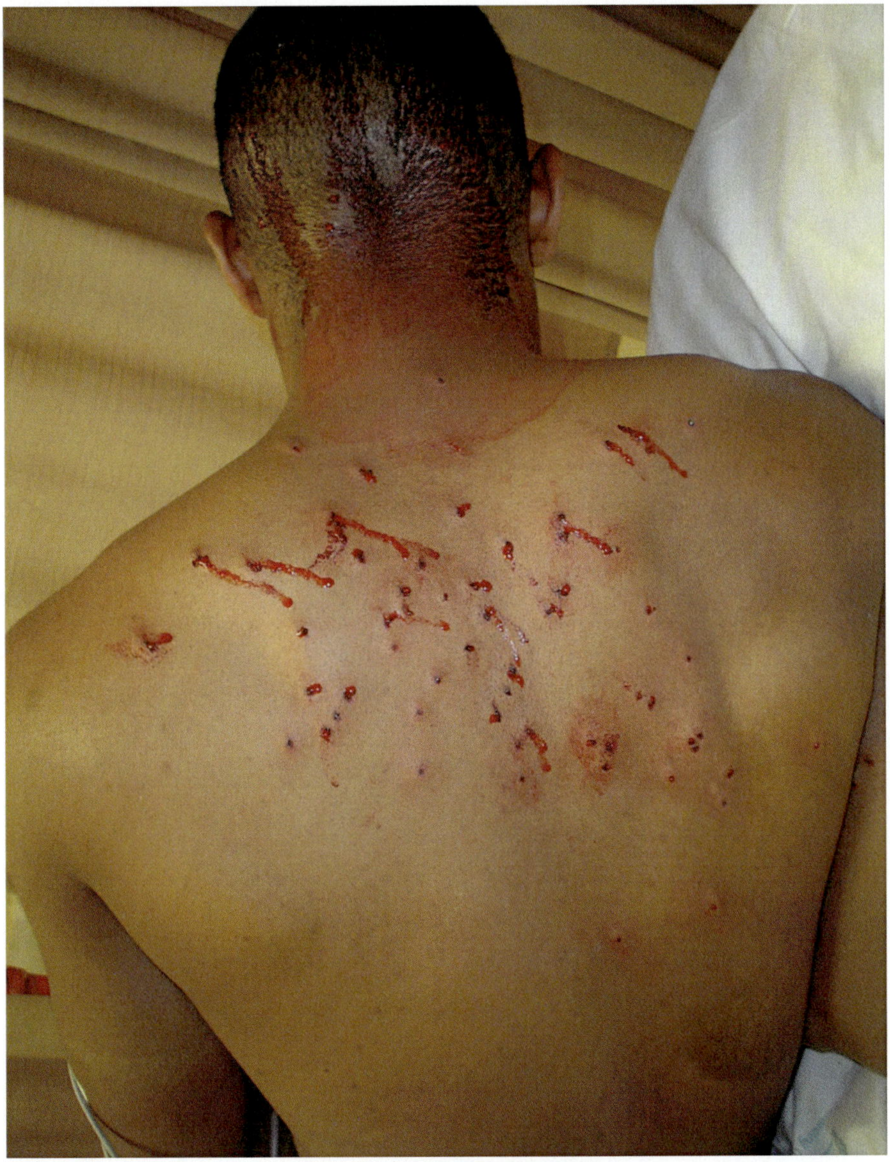

Shotgun wound to back.

Now consider a case in which an individual was hit by a shotgun at moderate distance from across a street. Do you think he survived? Absolutely, he survived!

None of the pellet rounds actually penetrated his skin. Due to the distance and subsequent loss of kinetic energy, none of the pellets had enough force to penetrate the thick skin of this individual's back. The skin layers on the human back, which include fat and connective tissue, can be up to a quarter inch or thicker on some individuals. Therefore, this gentleman went home after some hours, as soon as the assigned medical student finished plucking out the lead pellets from his back.

Let's look at yet another case. A man is carjacked and subsequently hit by a shotgun round in the left side of his face, below his jaw. He also takes a hit in the left shoulder from a slug and in the right forearm from small-gauge buckshot.

Are such injuries survivable? Yes, they are all survivable! Is he still in the fight? Yes, he is!

In fact, the individual actually managed to drive his car to the nearby hospital and park it in the lot. He even walked from his car into the emergency department on his own. We promptly put him to sleep and gave him a tracheostomy to protect his airway in anticipation of emergency surgery and presumed swelling.

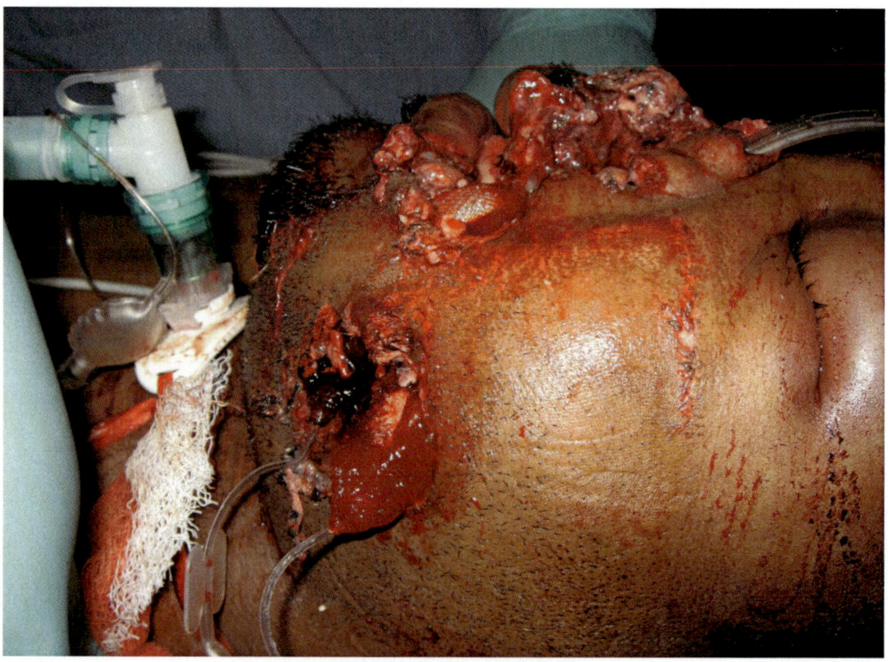

Shotgun wound to face.

Despite all the reconstructive surgery required to put his face back together, the man survived. His shoulder posed less of a repair problem. His arm, however, required more extensive reconstruction.

How about this case in which a police officer shot an offender in the back of the neck? The bullet entered through the back right side of the

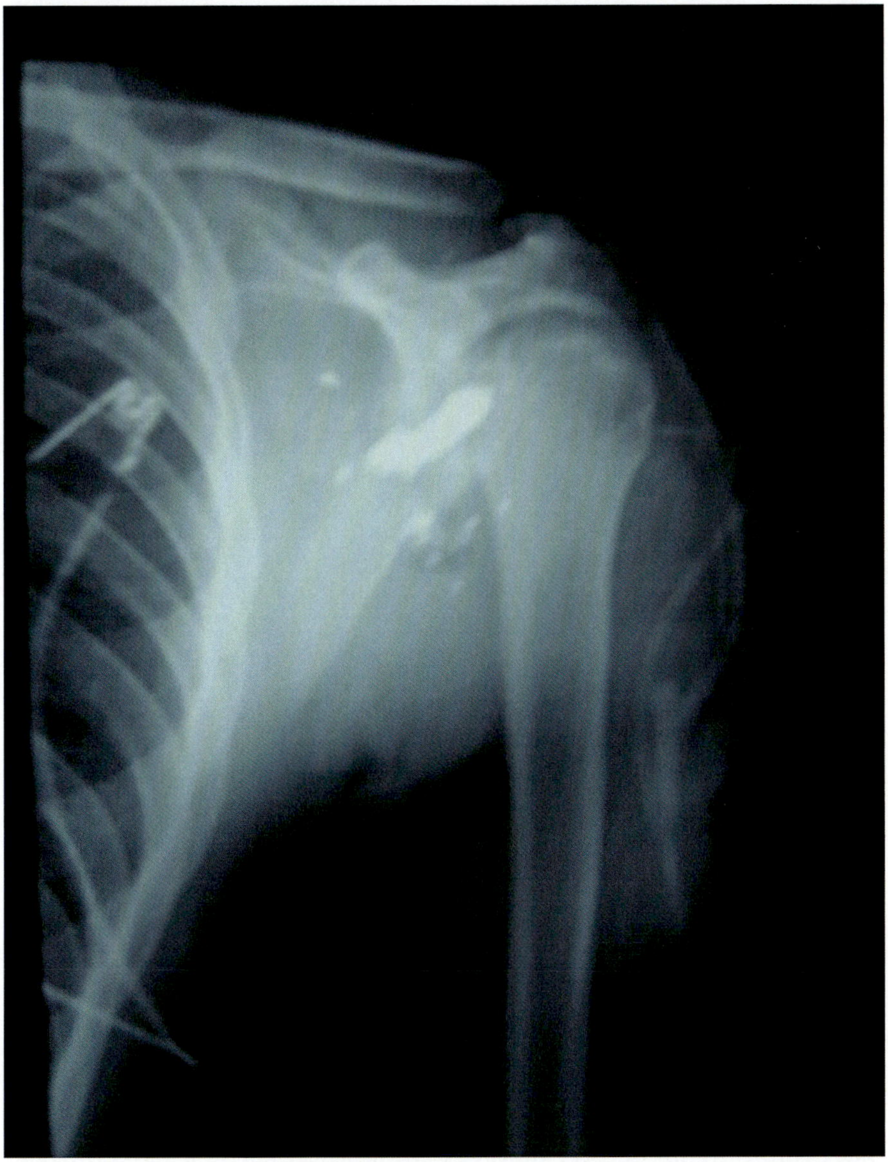

Shotgun wound to shoulder.

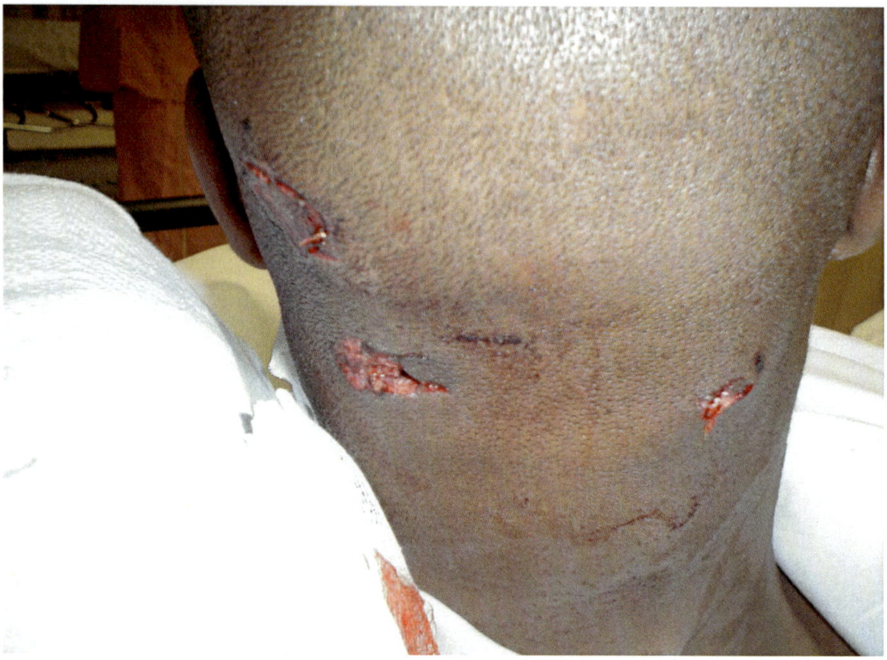

Gunshot wound to back of neck.

individual's neck and exited out through the left side of the neck. Did the offender survive? Yes, he did.

The bullet passed through the soft tissues of the man's neck. CT scans of his neck and head were all negative. He was therefore discharged from the trauma unit and transferred to lockup.

In another case, a male offender sustained multiple gunshot wounds to the torso in the right side of his back and right lower buttocks.

Are his wounds survivable? Yes, they are.

Is he still in the fight and still a threat? Absolutely!

A closer examination of the wounds revealed that there were no organs at risk, and the associated bleeding and pain were both minimal.

Reflecting on the various wound cases discussed throughout the chapter thus far, it should be noted that bleeding from most gunshot wounds is typically quite minimal.

This is in sharp contrast to the fictionalized shooting scenes acted out on Hollywood TV and movie sets.

Moving on, let's take a look at the different types of body tissues and their strategic importance in determining wounding. Body tissues that exhibit higher density tend to exhibit lower elasticity. In contrast, body tissues that exhibit lower density tend to exhibit higher elasticity.

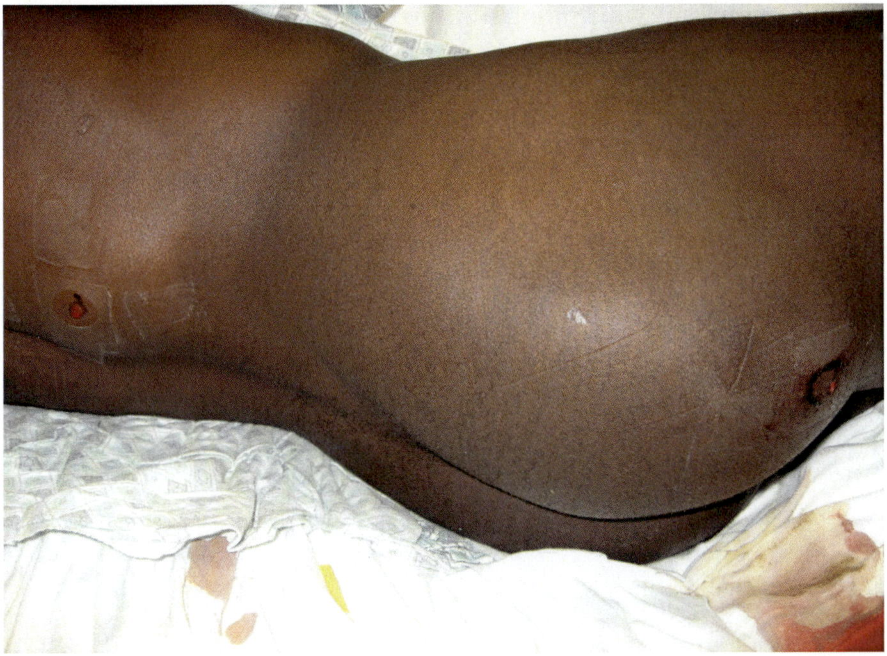

Gunshot wounds to back and buttocks.

Note the terms "density" and "elasticity" we used here to convey the tissue's characteristics and ability to accommodate energy transfer and resulting injury.

Starting with *bone,* it exhibits high density and low elasticity. Bone will typically fracture, or break apart, in response to being struck by a bullet, as it is incapable of absorbing the energy transferred upon impact.

Brain tissue also exhibits high density and low elasticity. The brain is similar in consistency to the yolk of a hard-boiled egg. With little capacity for absorbing energy, the tissue breaks into pieces upon impact.

Liver tissue also exhibits high density and low elasticity. The liver is similar in consistency to an intact shell-less, hard-boiled egg. The overall structure of the liver is composed of blood channels that contain blood vessels. The liver has some ability to absorb small amounts of energy but will typically crack on impact, resulting in bleeding.

In contrast to bone, brain, and liver tissue, *lung* tissue exhibits relatively low density and high elasticity. Soft and squishy in texture, the lungs possess a sponge-like ability to absorb large amounts of kinetic energy on impact with minimal injury, other than the creation of a permanent cavity.

As with lung tissue, both *muscle* and *heart* tissue also exhibit low density and high elasticity. Because the heart is a muscle, it is also somewhat capable of stretching and absorbing energy.

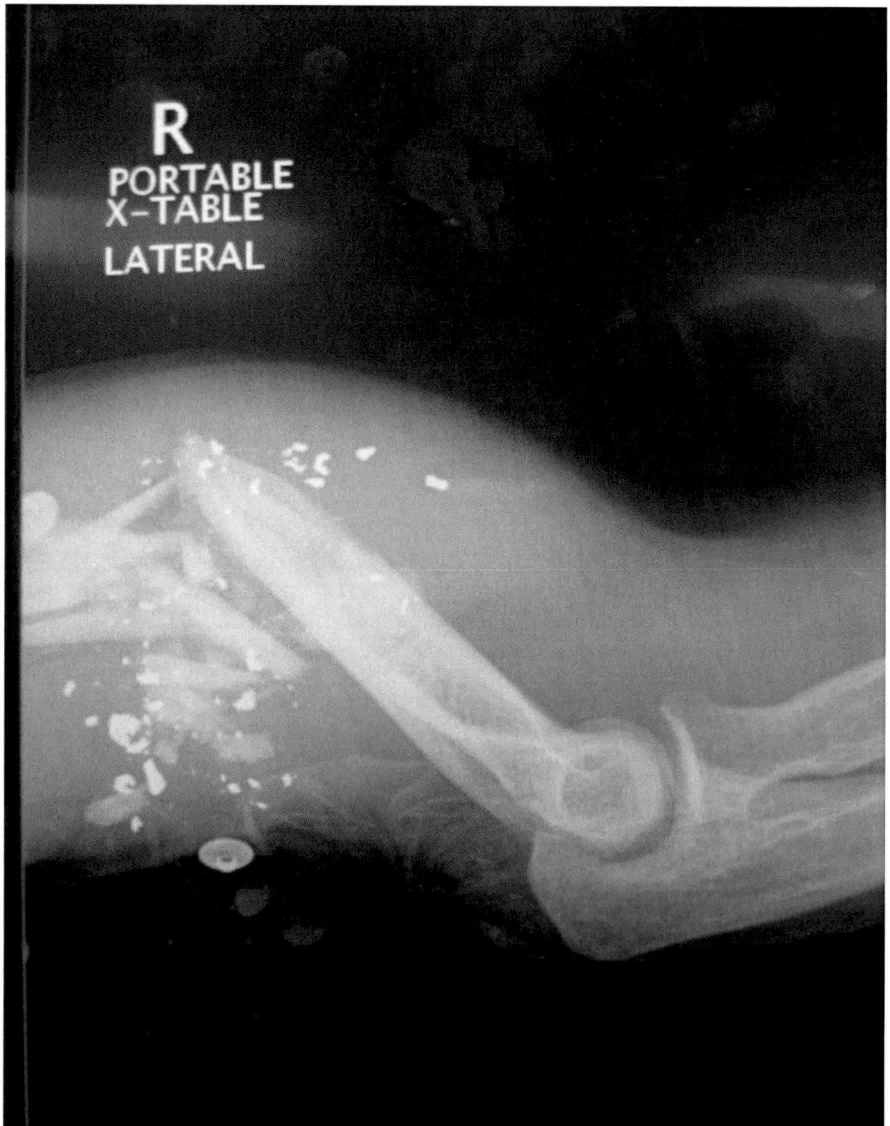

Broken bone from gunshot wound.

Earlier, we referenced the heart as a fluid-filled vessel constructed of muscle capable of stretching. When the valves to the heart are closed, the heart becomes a four-chamber, closed, fluid-filled container. If it is struck by a bullet, how do you think the heart will react?

If you guessed poorly, you are correct! As a fluid-filled container, the fluid, or blood, is non-compressible; and when subjected to kinetic energy, the fluid will be displaced and forced out through the path of least resistance. In this case, it is the fresh hole made by the bullet. Hence, ballistic-penetrating injuries to the heart usually are catastrophic, resulting in significant tissue damage that is frequently lethal.

Interestingly, the bladder, on the other hand, reacts differently. The bladder is also a closed, fluid-filled container but, unlike the heart, it is capable of stretching significantly on a regular basis. Hence, it is far more compliant and able to absorb the displacement caused by cavitation.

What about a stab wound to the heart? Does a stab wound behave similarly to a gunshot wound to the heart?

Actually, the two types of wounds behave quite differently. Stab sounds, by nature, are very low velocity, and therefore are associated with no cavitation. With respect to the heart, if a knife penetrates the

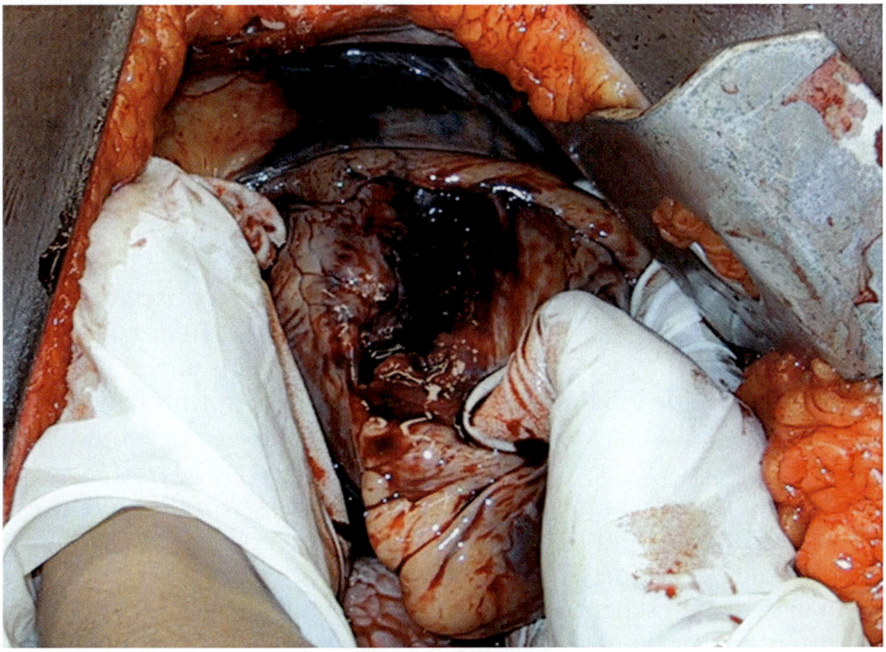

Gunshot wound to heart.

chest into the heart, it must get through the chest wall, often the lung, and then through the pericardial sac around the heart, and then into the heart.

The heart is encased in a protective, thick fibrous sac called the pericardium. If a blade penetrates the pericardial sac into the heart muscle, bleeding will occur and begin to fill the sac. The hole in the sac will frequently fill with blood, then clot and seal, but the heart will continue to bleed. As the blood clots, it becomes like grape jelly in consistency.

As the sac fills up with so much blood and clots, it begins to limit the space that the heart muscle has to effectively expand to enable its pumping action. Thus, the heart becomes increasingly deficient and, eventually, no longer capable of pumping at all. When this occurs the patient progresses into shock, and soon the heart stops, and the patient goes into cardiac arrest.

When a patient presents to a trauma center in either the early or late stages of this type of event and it is recognized, the trauma surgeon rapidly opens the patient's chest and then the pericardial sac to release the pressure or "tamponade" around the heart, allowing the heart to resume its pumping function. Next, the surgeon rapidly staples or sews up the hole in the heart, and the patient is given blood and fluids as necessary and taken to the operating room to have his chest washed out and closed up.

Such events may happen in the trauma unit three to four times per year, and patients frequently do very well, leaving the hospital in a matter of days. Therefore, it is these types of seemingly miraculous cases of survival that demonstrate both the resilience of the human body and the critical importance of getting the injured victim to a definitive trauma center as soon as possible.

For those of you who remember Steve Irwin, the crocodile hunter, based on my reading of the occurrence, it was likely a pericardial tamponade that killed him. According to reports Irwin was impaled through the heart by the barbed tail of a sting ray. It is unclear whether he pulled it out or whether the sting ray pulled it out. But had the tail been left in his chest and removed later by surgeons, he would have likely survived the injury. If he did actually pull the barbed tail from his chest, it would have unplugged the hole in his heart and caused severe bleeding into the fluid-filled sac around the heart and, eventually, a pericardial tamponade.

So in the larger scheme of wounding and ballistics, the concern over density of target tissue essentially revolves around bullet retardation. Tissue density is the most significant property influencing bullet retar-

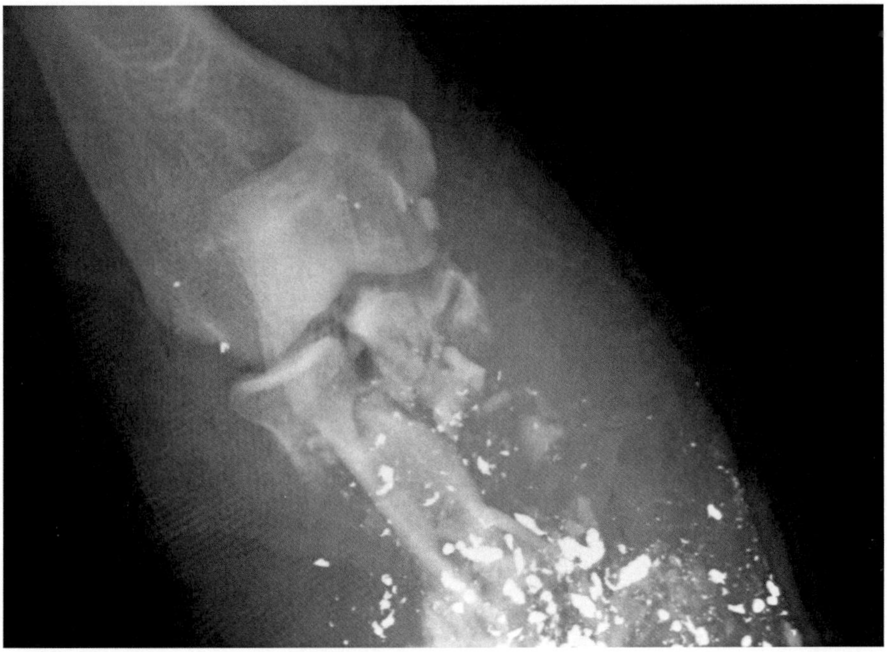

Shotgun wound to arm.

dation. The more dense the tissue, the greater the resistance it will pose against a penetrating projectile, such as a bullet. The greater the resistance, the greater the reduction in velocity, the greater the transfer of energy into the target body tissue and, hence, the more significant the overall wound site and cavity produced.

Let's also revert back for a moment to consider the man who was carjacked and shot in the face. The shot met with the high density bone tissue, resulting in extensive fractures.

How about the shot he also suffered to his right arm from either a birdshot or small-gauge buckshot at close range? The shot essentially produced a "lead snowstorm" effect in his arm. Unable to absorb the kinetic energy transferred with the shot, the bone essentially blew apart into multiple fragments and out the opposite side of the arm, resulting in devastating injury to the soft tissue.

As yet another example, what about an individual who sustained a single gunshot wound which fractured the left hip? The shot penetrated the soft tissue of the buttocks into the high density bone tissue, fracturing and displacing the left hip. Was this wound life threatening? No, and the offender still posed a threat, although most likely a stationary threat. Walking on a broken hip is unlikely.

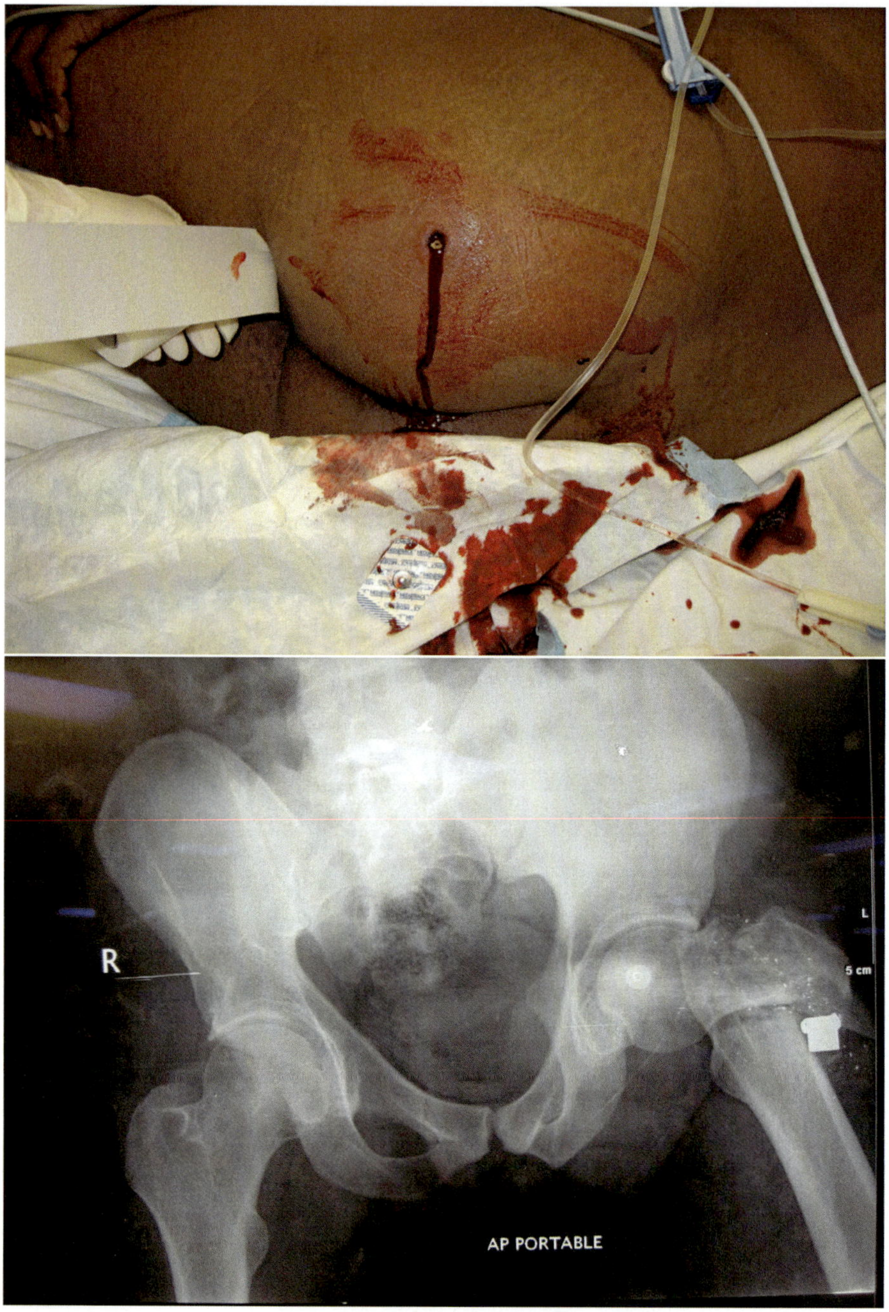

Hip fracture from gunshot.

Also worth mention was the relatively small amount of bleeding from the bullet hole in the left buttocks. The bleeding was not arterial in nature. Rather, it consisted of a slow venous ooze from the broken bone, decompressing out through the bullet hole. A majority of gunshot wounds, in fact, bleed minimally to the exterior.

What is the strategic importance to this injury? A cracked hip generally prohibits a person from walking or running away. The individual goes from being a much harder-to-hit moving target to a much easier-to-hit stationary target, explaining the rationale behind why many law enforcement agencies today teach officers to target the lateral pelvis in shooting to stop.

We have devoted much attention up to this point on the matter of tissue density. But what about the strategic importance of *tissue elasticity* in determining wounding?

As elasticity increases, kinetic energy absorption likewise increases. Consequently, tissue damage decreases. Conversely, as elasticity decreases, kinetic energy absorption likewise decreases. Consequently, tissue damage increases. In essence, it is the combination of shearing, compression, and stretching that ultimately determine the extent of a wound.

As previously mentioned, the lungs are an example of a less dense, yet more elastic, tissue. Due to their sponge-like quality, the lungs can absorb tremendous amounts of energy and thus sustain minimal tissue damage as a result.

The liver, on the other hand, is a rather inelastic tissue. Remember, the liver has the consistency of a hard-boiled egg with the softer inner yolk encapsulated by the stronger, protective white structure minus the outer hard shell. Similarly, the liver has a clear capsule-like structure. Incapable of accommodating energy transference, the liver will easily crack upon impact. Moreover, the liver comprises a complex mass of blood vessels. Consequently, any cracking of the organ will produce significant bleeding.

Let's look at another example in which a young woman was shot with a .45 Automatic Pistol in the right medial thigh. Upon exiting the thigh, the bullet left behind its copper jacket component embedded in her skin.

Was this leg injury life threatening? No. Although at first glance, the wound tract could be considered to cross the path of the major, or femoral, artery and vein of the leg. In this case, there was minimal external bleeding and, ultimately, no damage was done to the femoral artery and vein of the leg.

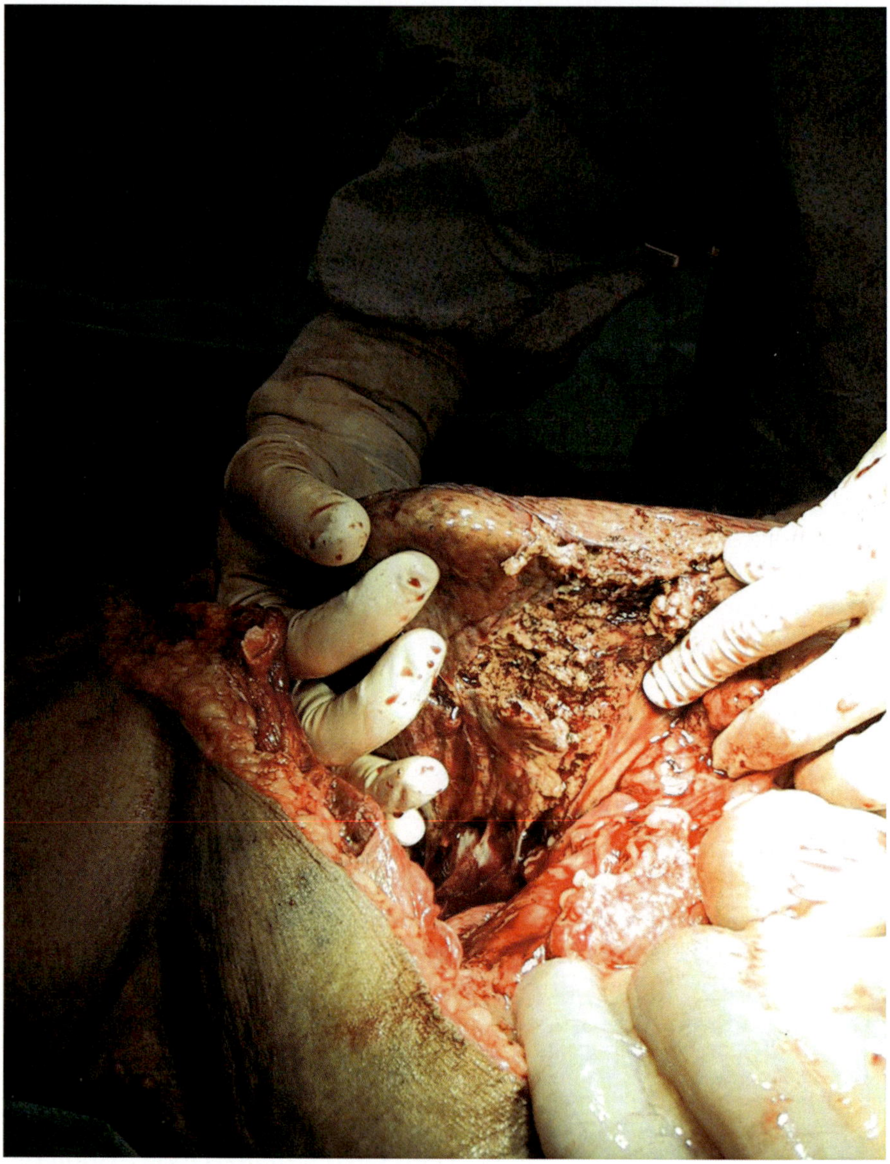

Cracked liver.

Nature strategically buried all of the big vascular pipes, or vital blood vessels, within our limbs for greater protection. The big pipes tend to run very deep and more central to the body along the inner side or along the bones of your arms and legs.

In the case of the woman struck in the thigh, the entrance hole was very close to the exit hole from which the bullet jacket was removed.

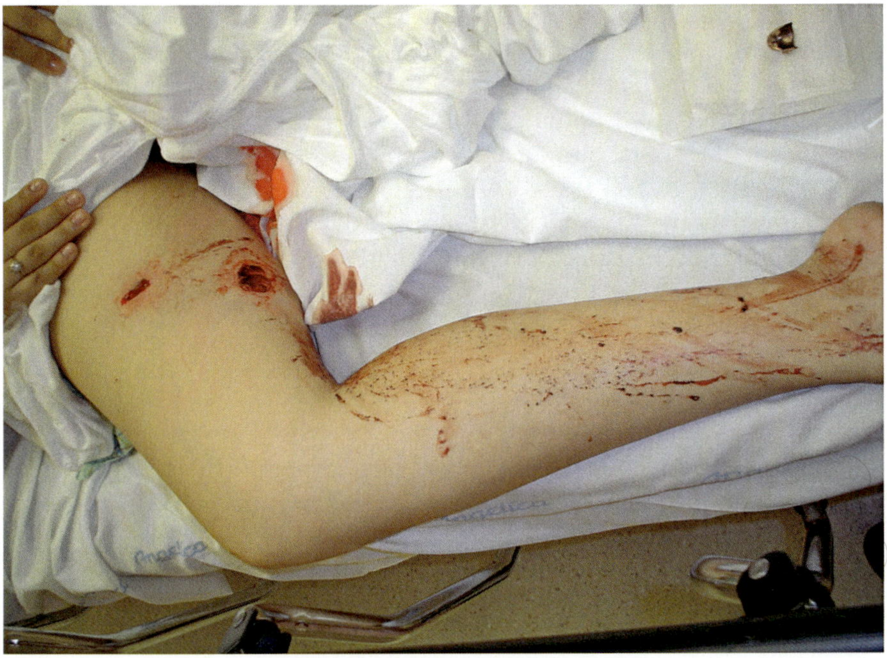

Gunshot wound to medial thigh.

Because of the proximity of the bullet entrance and exit, the risk of injury to the deep-lying femoral vessels was unlikely.

Managing such an injury until emergency department care can be received simply requires the application of a minimal amount of direct pressure. A tourniquet is likely unnecessary since there is no active, significant hemorrhaging, or bleeding.

Let's take a look at another scenario in which an individual is struck by a high-velocity round to the medial thigh. How would you manage such a massive leg injury out in the street? A tourniquet applied above the leg wound could help stop the acute blood-flow loss, although it may be overkill if the bleeding is not from a large artery. When one applies a tourniquet, one assumes total limb loss may occur.

A tourniquet essentially serves to create a tight band around a bleeding artery to help tie off and squeeze it closed. While a tourniquet may sometimes be necessary in cases of severe bleeding, its tight squeezing action may in turn cause further tissue damage.

Applying a pressure dressing, or *Emergency Bandage,* over the area of the leg wound instead would likely prove as sufficient in controlling the blood loss and serve as a better first-aid choice in this case. The

Emergency Bandage, also commonly known in U. S. and international military units as an "Israeli battle dressing" or "Israeli bandage," is designed to distribute the necessary amount of pressure more evenly over the wound site, helping to effectively control bleeding without causing further tissue damage.

The Trauma Rapid Intervention Kit (TRIK), developed for use in conjunction with the MTLE training program, is equipped with an *Israeli bandage.* This special type of highly versatile and indispensable bandage utilizes a "reverse-wrapping" technique to more evenly apply pressure to the wound site in helping to control bleeding, and can be applied using one hand.

The Israeli bandage contained within the TRIK can serve as an essential life-saving tool out in the street or other pre-hospital setting. The bandage can help effectively manage bleeding from almost any part of the body. In addition to providing compression, the bandage may be tightened to serve as a tourniquet for controlling more severe blood loss or as a supportive sling for a limb injury.

As discussed in the prior chapter on "mindset," remember that surviving and prevailing in a life-threatening situation in the street also depends largely on your ability to control your associated fear and maintain a rational and tactical state of mind under pressure. Understanding the different types of injuries that typically occur out in the

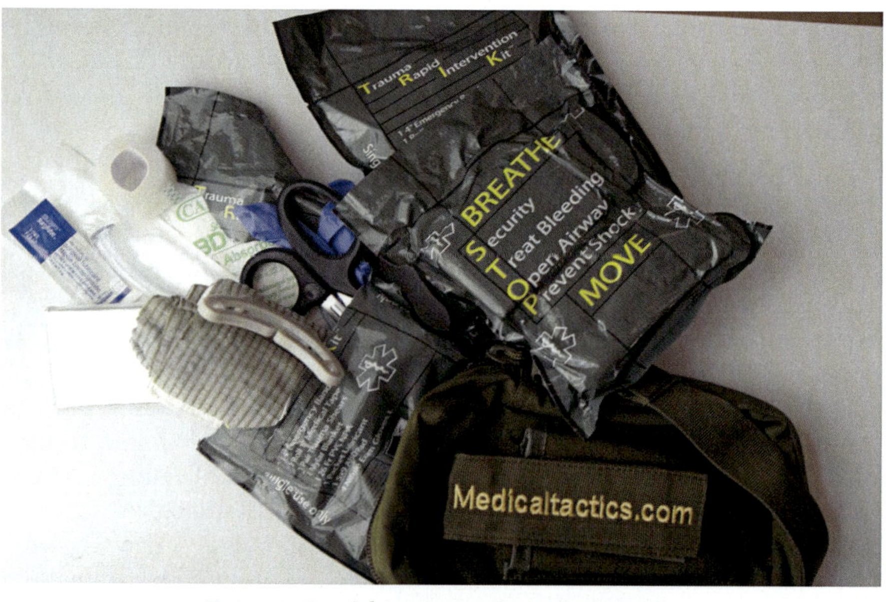

Trauma Rapid Intervention Kit (TRIK).

street is critical to also understanding the associated disabilities and practical skills for applying life-saving medical tactics. By developing this knowledge, you can help minimize the risk of panic, improve decision making, and ultimately increase the chances for achieving a favorable outcome.

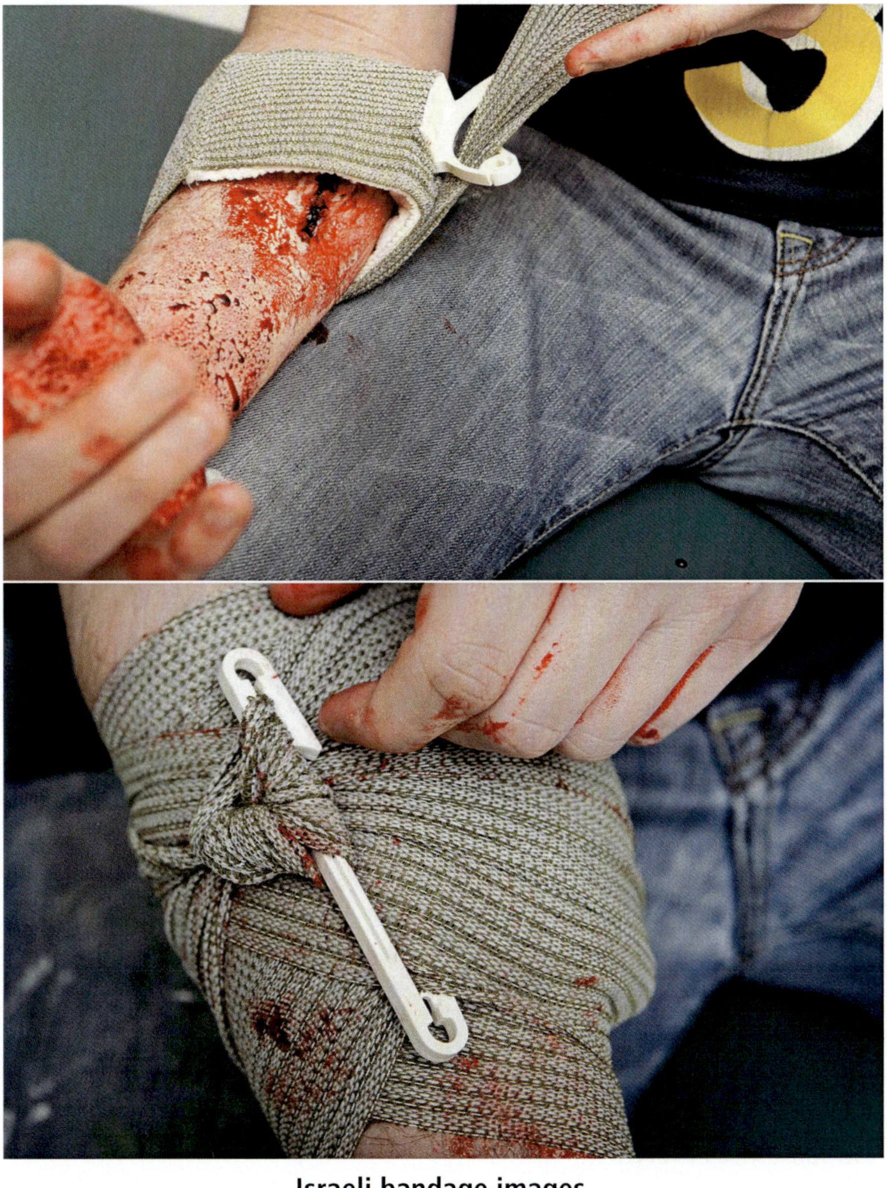

Israeli bandage images.

Fear can prove to be a costly distraction to survival. But if you can effectively manage your fear in a situation, you can better control your mind and body to stay in the fight. You can then effectively apply life-saving tactics, including: directing your defensive assaults against the offender's vulnerable anatomy; anticipating a disability and maintaining your ability to function, such as reloading and shooting your firearm with an injured hand; and carrying injured victims to safety.

After all, the odds of survival are on your side! To help keep things in perspective, consider that a bullet is a very small projectile, often measuring less than an inch and therefore posing a relatively small chance of actually striking a vital organ or vessel. Only about one in six is killed by gunfire, according to a report published by The University of Chicago Crime Lab (Ander, Cook, Ludwig, and Pollack, 2009). Keep in mind that this statistic includes civilians without body armor.

Moreover, the human body by nature is rather well designed to protect itself from injury. For instance, vital organs such as the heart, liver, and spleen are protected by the rib cage. The big vascular pipes of the body are all centrally buried deep within the core. The big pipes of the limbs are located along the inner side nearer the midline of the body and along the bones. When a vessel is injured it spasms to limit blood loss. Surrounding tissues act as barriers to limit blood loss and eventually, if blood pressure falls, bleeding slows down. All are nature's way of enhancing survival.

Consider, for instance, what happens when a bone beaks within the body? How does the body typically respond? The body contracts the muscles around the bone. This spasm effect is essentially nature's way of applying a temporary splint to immobilize the bone and help reduce the risk of further injury.

When an injury causes bones to rub together, pain results from the friction and serves as a signal to the body to maintain a protective stance. The body then instinctively reacts to protect the injured limb by drawing it in close to the torso.

When a major blood vessel is injured, such as the femoral artery that runs along the inside of the leg, how does the body typically respond? The body's natural response is to help minimize blood loss by shrinking the diameter of the injured artery through spasm, or contraction. As the diameter of the artery shrinks and slows the blood flow from the damaged artery, clots form to help further minimize or stop the bleeding. Blood that moves slowly stands still or encounters turbulence clots. Hence a vessel spasms, the rate of blood flow slows, and therefore clots form.

Remember, most of the wounds discussed throughout this chapter were characterized by a relatively minimal amount of bleeding. While many types of wounds may produce bleeding, most gunshot wounds tend to bleed minimally from the entrance or exit wounds.

By better understanding how the body naturally responds on its own to life-threatening injury, you can then also effectively learn to apply the medical tactics, or life-saving set of "scripted" steps—BREATHE, STOP, MOVE—introduced in the prior chapter. The next couple of chapters are devoted to further developing your understanding of how this fundamental script can serve to help define your response to life-threatening injury, and ultimately improve your chances of survival in the street.

CHAPTER 4

MANAGEMENT

ASSESSMENT AND INTERVENTION IN BALANCING MEDICAL LIFE-SAVING AND MISSION PRIORITIES

The previous chapter of this book served to help you develop a foundation of knowledge on the mechanics of penetrating trauma. In this chapter, we will build on this foundation through learning about the importance of appropriate assessment and intervention as taught and emphasized in the MTLE training program.

In essence, when you are out in the street and a life-threatening situation is unfolding, you must quickly determine *what* to do and *when* to do it in balancing life-saving measures, tactics, and mission priorities. Consider this hypothetical scenario in which you are tasked with responding to a shots fired call from a fellow officer. You are the first officer to arrive on the scene and spot two victims who have both just been shot and are lying on the ground in an alley in plain view.

There are puddles of blood surrounding both victims. One of the victims is a police officer. The armed offender is visible. The narrow alley with limited escape options presents a "fatal funnel" situation. You must quickly assess the situation and determine your intervention response. The types of high-stress conditions presented with this scenario are among the major reasons underlying the development of the MTLE training program and pre-scripted response—BREATHE, STOP, MOVE.

Remember, we explained earlier how scripts, or algorithms, can effectively guide our decision making under such pressure-cooker situations. Life-saving decisions in the street therefore do not have to be so hard after all. Let's see how this works by reviewing each step of the MTLE script BREATHE, STOP, MOVE more closely.

BREATHE, before you do anything! Take this critical timeout to gain control over the situation and prioritize your actions. Remember to perform the dynamic tactical breathing technique introduced earlier. Taking some forced, or deliberate, breaths will help to slow down your heart rate and enable you to focus on controlling your physical and mental stress, including your fear. To BREATHE is always your first step and cannot be overstated. There is always time to gain control of yourself and of the situation.

The second step in the MTLE script is to STOP! The S-T-O-P step breaks down into four key substeps: S-ecure the situation, T-reat bleeding, O-pen airway, and P-revent shock.

S-ecure the situation by first performing a quick SCAN. What does this substep entail exactly? Performing a S-C-A-N in essence comprises four key actions: S-urveil area, C-ontrol variables, A-ssess goals and N-ever lose sight of the threat! In essence, you must determine what is beyond your control, and what is within your control. Then based on what you can control, quickly assess your options and determine your goals for surviving and prevailing in the situation, all the while keeping your eyes on the threat.

More specifically, *surveil area* involves identifying any injured victims and possible threats on the scene. After identifying the injured, you will need to consider whether the situation warrants the need to perform victim rescues or body recoveries. Does the benefit of performing a rescue or recovery outweigh the risk? How can you determine what steps to take?

Perform the *remote victim assessment* technique. Start by confirming that the injured victim is still breathing. Simply ask the victim to provide a verbal response. One of the earliest signs of shock is confusion, indicating that the brain may be lacking oxygen. If the victim is unable to verbally respond, determine if you can see the rise and fall of his chest to confirm that he is still breathing.

Simultaneously, look for any spontaneous movements. This remote assessment allows the rescuer to confirm that the victim is, in fact, still alive. If not, then the effort no longer requires a rescue, and all of the urgency is gone.

Once you have performed the remote victim assessment, determine how you can *control the variables* of the situation. The first variable addresses what goals you must accomplish to survive and prevail in the situation. The second variable addresses how you can help minimize the risks to yourself as well as the injured victims or others involved on the scene in accomplishing these goals.

After you have determined how to control the variables, the next action point is to *assess goals.* To survive and prevail in a life-threatening situation, you must focus on three key goals:

1. take cover to conceal yourself and any victims from the offender,
2. eliminate the threat, and
3. extract yourself and the victims from the hot zone to safety.

In planning your extraction route, consider vulnerable points along the way that could put you in the offender's direct line of sight and expose you to attack. If you need to assist, drag, or carry a victim along the route to safety, consider whether you can realistically manage the distance and travel time. Do you plan to escape via the same route from which you entered the scene?

Whatever the situation, remember: *never lose sight* of the looming threat, apply strategic survival tactics before medical treatment, and prepare to adapt!

Once you have managed to *S-ecure* the situation, it's time to move on to the second sub-step of S-T-O-P, which is to *T-reat bleeding.* Thus, it's helpful to gain a basic understanding of bleeding and what you can treat out in the street.

First off, bleeding control at this time should be limited to extreme cases of bleeding only. Unless a bleed is actively spurting like a fountain and creating a puddle of blood or soaking the victim's clothes like he was in a swimming pool, there is no need to address it at this time.

While bleeding can be visually distressing, its management, when required, is actually very straightforward. The trick is to think of it as no more complicated than plumbing. The blood vessels running throughout the body are akin to the water pipes running throughout your home or other buildings, and the heart is akin to a water pump.

Blood flows upstream to the heart where it cycles through and gets pumped right back out to the rest of the body, including downstream all the way through to the tips of your fingers and toes. In effect, your heart serves the vital function of keeping a freshly oxygenated, nourishing blood supply circulating throughout the vessels of your body.

So the ways in which you would repair a leaking blood vessel in the body are relatively similar in theory and practice to how you would repair a leaking water pipe at home. When a pipe, or vessel, springs a leak, the fluid no longer runs downstream and is simply lost to the environment. The goal is to keep it within the piping system.

The primary goals for treating bleeding are therefore two-fold: prevent further blood loss and restore downstream blood flow. In terms of what you can feasibly treat in the street, you can treat bleeding from the head, arms, and legs.

Treating bleeding from the abdomen and chest is much more difficult in the street, as it is frequently internal and not amendable to external control. Depending on the degree of blood loss, you may need to plan for an especially swift extraction of the victim to the safe zone for immediate transportation to the nearest trauma center.

To confirm downstream blood flow in the injured victim, you can check the peripheral pulse on the underside of the victim's wrist. You can also check the efficiency of capillary refilling by simply pressing firmly on one of the victim's fingernails and then releasing the finger and counting the number of seconds for return of normal tissue color under the fingernail.

Before we review the possible interventions for treating bleeding, it's important to first understand that *no one* should die from bleeding of the extremities. Extremity bleeding is 100 percent treatable out in the street, so the number of casualties can and should be 0 percent.

Yet interestingly, 10 percent of military battlefield casualties in the Vietnam conflict were estimated to have died from uncontrolled extremity bleeding, according to a study published in a 2005 issue of the Journal of TRAUMA® Injury, Infection, and Critical Care (Dorlac, DeBakey, Holcomb, Fagan, Kwong, Dorlac, Schreiber, Persse, Moore, and Mattox, 2005). Much to our relief, the study results published in the journal did not show a correlation between the Vietnam statistic and civilian injuries in recent times.

As further illustration, the Wound Data and Munitions Effectiveness Team (1970) reported that 2,500 U. S. soldiers were lost in Vietnam due to isolated extremity issues. Meanwhile, less than 1 percent was reportedly lost due to airway compromise.

Determining which method to use to treat bleeding injuries in the street requires that you develop an understanding of the principles of pressure. There are three basic sets of principles of pressure. Let's take a look at the first set.

Principles of Pressure I: "Remember, it's all about plumbing." Revisiting the pipe metaphor, remember the key is to fix the leak and, if possible, preserve downstream blood flow. To patch a smaller pipe or vessel leak, you can simply apply direct pressure to the wound with a gloved finger—always the first step. If that doesn't suffice to stop the bleeding, then you can apply a pressure dressing or tourniquet.

How does the direct pressure principle work? To control a bleeding vessel, the inward pressure applied against the wounded vessel must be greater than the outward pressure of the blood flow. As the bleeding vessel is compressed inward against bone, the downstream blood flow is effectively reduced but frequently not completely eliminated.

Unfortunately, pressure has its limitations, especially in the torso where all the large blood vessels lie deep within the core. Here it is very difficult to focus and direct the pressure to the likely areas of bleeding.

Additionally, one runs the risk of doing greater harm since compressing the abdomen or chest can compromise breathing. The neck is also a tricky area to control bleeding as constriction around the neck may stop bleeding, but it will likely also compromise the airway and potentially inhibit uninjured blood vessels from providing blood to the brain. Hence, you can't use a pressure dressing to treat a neck wound as it could constrict blood flow to the victim's brain or collapse his windpipe, proving fatal. Instead, you can apply manual direct pressure to the neck wound, using a hand.

Will applying the *Principles of Pressure I*—direct pressure or a pressure dressing—effectively control bleeding in all cases of extremity

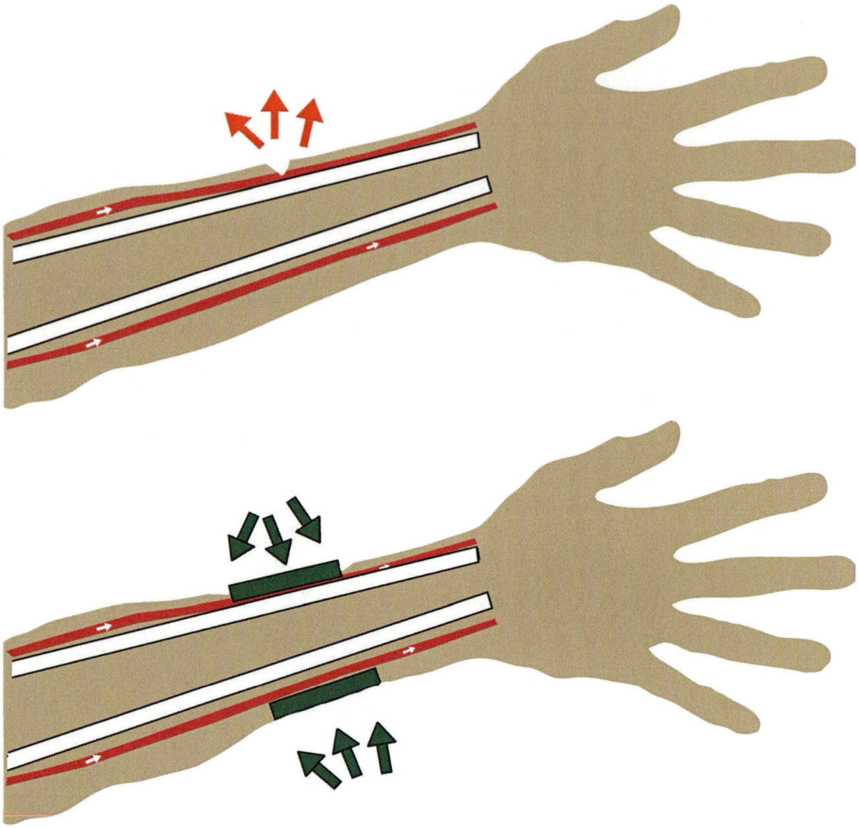

Principles of pressure applied to arm.

injury? No. While these options will work to effectively control bleeding in a majority of situations, some cases require more attention. Let's take a look at the next set of principles of pressure.

Principles of Pressure II: "Direct pressure where it is most needed." In deep, actively bleeding cavity injuries, external surface pressure alone may not be sufficient to control bleeding. To be effective, the pressure applied must be directed precisely where it is needed. This is achieved by filling any space between the bleeding vessel and the area of applied pressure so that the force can be directed to where it is needed. In the medical field, this type of pressure application is known as "wound packing."

So how do you pack a wound? You fill the entire wound with the best available material, preferably the medical gauze contained in the Trauma Rapid Intervention Kit (TRIK). The key to controlling bleeding in a deep wound is to extend the applied pressure all the way to the

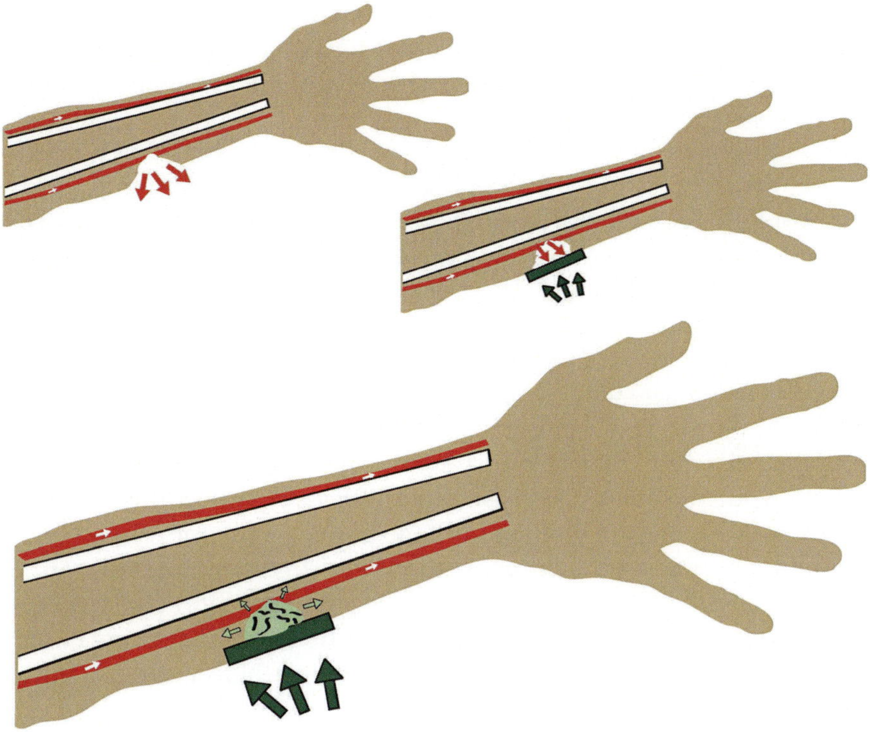

Wound packing.

bottom of the wound. Packing the wound therefore enables you to direct the surface pressure through the depth of the wound.

Let's revisit the pipe metaphor again for a moment to help illustrate. Imagine that a water main ruptures under the street near your home. Do you think you could fix the broken water main by simply placing a plate or shield over the surface of the street? No. The broken main will continue to leak water under the street. Instead, workmen will need to dig a hole, expose the pipe and apply a repair patch to the source.

Packing is particularly useful for treating deep wounds in which a chunk of flesh is missing. For this type of wound, crumple the packing material as tightly as possible. The crumpled packing material will expand to fill the wound, applying more pressure against the source leak.

Once you have packed the wound, you can then apply a pressure dressing over the top to further increase and help maintain the pressure. The pressure dressing forces the packing material into the wound, which helps to direct the pressure all the way to the bottom of the wound.

Exceptions for packing deep wounds are the chest and abdomen. Packing is generally ineffective in these instances as it is too difficult to effectively direct the pressure precisely where it is needed to control bleeding. The large vessels of the chest and abdomen are too deep to reach with packing material, and the spaces of the chest and abdomen are too vast.

What happens when the *Principles of Pressure I and II* combined—that is, direct pressure and a pressure dressing combined with packing the wound—are still not enough to get the bleeding under control? Some more serious wounds require a more dramatic intervention approach. Fortunately, there are still more options for treating bleeding that can be applied in the street.

Principles of Pressure III: "Apply a tourniquet as an emergency shut-off valve." Say you apply a patch in an attempt to repair and control a water pipe leak, but the water just keeps on leaking through the patch. What's your next move? If you can't effectively get control over the problem downstream, you shut off the main water supply upstream.

Similar to the pipe metaphor, the blood loss from certain injuries must be completely shut off upstream to prevent fatal consequences. One option is to apply packing upstream of the injury, using enough pressure to completely compress the leaking blood vessels inward against the underlying bone

In some cases, however, certain injuries will require a tourniquet to control the bleeding. With an amputated limb injury, for instance, the large, exposed tissue surface area has too many vessels actively bleeding and is frequently accompanied by an open, severed end of a large vessel. In severed limbs, the outward blood flow is simply too great for direct pressure to stop the loss. Hence, we go for shutting off the main supply.

What does a large blood vessel, or arterial, bleed look like? You will see copious, bright red blood often spurting or spraying out in pulses from the wound site.

What is a tourniquet exactly, and how does it work to control excessive blood loss? A tourniquet is similar in principle to a pressure dressing applied upstream of an injury to cut off the downstream blood flow.

A tourniquet should measure at least one-inch wide. The wider the better, as distributing the pressure more evenly across the tissues helps to reduce the risk of further damage. To be effective, the tourniquet must be applied upstream of the wound and tightly enough to completely shut off the blood flow downstream from the wound.

Considering that a tourniquet eliminates, rather than reduces, the blood flow, the downstream body tissues will no longer receive a nourishing blood supply. Isn't the total lack of blood flow potentially damaging to the downstream body tissue?

Yes, the lack of blood flow does cause tissue damage. So, you must consider whether the benefit of using the tourniquet to arrest blood loss outweighs the risk. Wherever one places a tourniquet, one must assume that the limb will be sacrificed from there down. Hence, it is always advisable to place the tourniquet upstream but as close to the wound as possible.

Whether to use a tourniquet will depend on the degree of blood loss associated with the injury and the situational environment. For instance, tourniquets are often used with great effectiveness on the military battlefield for treating serious blast and amputation injuries produced by explosive devices. Tourniquets are particularly essential when the blood loss can't be afforded with longer extraction times.

Also, keep in mind that tourniquet placement is very painful. The actual application of the device as well as the blood-starved limb will produce significant pain.

Relative to the use of tourniquets by police officers in the street, the majority of civilian injuries do not require this degree of intervention. Unlike the military battlefield, encounters with major explosive devices are not so likely for police officers in the street. Thus, applying direct pressure is often sufficient to control blood loss for most of the civilian injuries sustained in the street. This is not to say that a tourniquet does not have its place.

The previously referenced issue of *The Journal of TRAUMA®, Injury, Infection, and Critical Care* published the results of a five-and-a-half-year review of 95 percent of trauma admissions in Houston, TX, totaling more than 75,000 admissions. Only 14, or 0.2 percent, of the total admissions were considered exsanguinating, life-threatening extremity injuries. Fifty percent were attributed to gunshot wounds, and 71 percent were associated with the lower extremities. Despite resuscitation efforts, all of the patients died even though eight out of the 14, or 57 percent, had injuries that could have been controlled with a tourniquet (Dorlac et al., 2005).

There may also be a tactical advantage for police officers to use tourniquets in treating injuries with severe blood loss in the street. A tourniquet can be rapidly and easily applied in dynamic, life-threatening situations. Once in the safe zone, the tourniquet can be downgraded to a simple pressure dressing within a short period of time of less than an hour.

Up to this point, the interventions discussed for controlling bleeding out in the street have been mechanical in nature. However, there are also chemical interventions that are available for use to help control bleeding.

Principles of Pressure IV: "Hemostatic agents enhance the clotting capabilities of blood." A form of chemical intervention, a hemostatic agent can be added directly to a wound or preapplied to a pressure dressing or packing material used to treat the wound.

What to remember about bleeding:

1. Gunshot wounds often do *not* bleed externally.
2. Bright red, rapidly-spurting blood from a wound indicates more serious arterial bleeding.
3. External bleeding can usually be brought under control with the application of pressure.
4. The use of a tourniquet, although sometimes a critically necessary life-saving measure, can result in further limb damage or potentially even limb loss.

There are several types of hemostatic agents, and each works by a different mechanism. New agents are being developed all of the time, and many appear to show great promise.

However, it's important to understand that a hemostatic agent is not effective on its own! The agent must be combined with direct pressure and is most effective when applied along with a pressure dressing or packing material.

Be aware of expiration dates to help ensure effectiveness of the agent. Make a note of when you need to discard and replace the agent. Also note that there appears to be little data available that shows the use of hemostatic agents as effective in improving survival. These agents are still a relatively new medical intervention, so overwhelming supportive clinical data for their use simply isn't available yet.

Relative to all of the bleeding interventions discussed, there is no one perfect intervention. Direct pressure, pressure dressings, tourniquets, and hemostatic agents are all useful and effective in helping to control bleeding under certain circumstances. Let's take a look at the pros and cons of each technique.

The *direct pressure* technique uses a gloved hand or other object to apply pressure over the wound area. What are the *pros?* The technique is always readily available and quick and easy to apply, requiring just one hand and no tools other than a glove or material such as gauze to provide a protective barrier. What are the *cons?* The technique requires at least one hand to maintain constant pressure over the wound, making it harder to use when moving, and it requires a committed person to maintain the pressure.

The *pressure dressing* technique uses a bandage that applies constant, direct pressure over the wound area. What are the *pros?* The technique is highly versatile, stopping local bleeding without compromising the flow to other intact vessels of the extremity. What are the cons? One con is that the technique may be ineffective for injuries that produce severe bleeding.

The *tourniquet* technique is used to completely cut off blood flow to the wound area and extremity. What are the *pros?* The technique is relatively fast and easy to apply. What are the *cons?* Because the technique completely shuts off all blood flow to both the wound and through the end of the extremity, it also prevents blood from flowing through intact vessels and tissue. Thus, if left on too long it deprives the intact vessels and tissue of nourishing blood which can result in further damage to the injured limb or potentially even limb loss. As previously noted, tourniquets are also very painful when applied correctly.

The application of a *hemostatic agent* enhances clotting of the blood. What are the *pros?* The enhanced blood clotting slows the loss of blood from the wound. What are the *cons?* Such agents are not very effective as a stand-alone treatment for bleeding and must be used in conjunction with a pressure dressing over the wound.

Now that you have a fundamental understanding of how to treat bleeds, how likely do you think it is that you would survive a gunshot or stab wound in the street? Fortunately, the odds of surviving such a wound are in your favor! Without body armor, the survival rate is one in six. With body armor, one can only surmise that the survival rate improves.

Anecdotally, three in five people who suffer penetrating injury, whether a gunshot or stab wound, leave trauma centers after six hours. Therefore, an important factor to keep in mind when assessing an injury in the street is the human body's amazing resilience.

Of all of the steps for controlling bleeding, accurate injury assessment is the most crucial. Proper assessment can make a true life-saving difference. Applying pressure or gauze to an injury is not a cure-all. How do you know when an injury is life-threatening and requires more comprehensive, immediate care?

Consider these two different types of injuries: one is a laceration to the arm, and the other is a laceration to the abdomen. In both cases, the injuries appear to be fairly sizeable, measuring several inches in length and a few inches wide. The injuries are causing some bleeding, yet the muscles appear to be uncut. Would you consider these injuries to be life-threatening in nature, requiring immediate care? No. Why not? The injuries are not bleeding significantly, indicating the major vessels of the tissue are intact.

How would you treat these wounds? For the arm laceration, you would just apply direct pressure to the wound with a gloved hand and a protective bandage when convenient. The abdominal laceration just requires the application of a protective bandage when convenient.

The Trauma Rapid Intervention Kit (TRIK) is specifically designed with the street encounter in mind. The TRIK is equipped with essentials for treating the various types of bleeding injuries discussed which are typical of street situations. What options for bleeding control are in the TRIK?

Among the greatest pre-hospital bleeding control interventions, the Emergency Bandage, also known as the "Israeli Battle Dressing," serves as a highly versatile pressure dressing or tourniquet. There is no need to reapply the bandage for tourniquet conversion. The bandage is easily adjusted in the street. Simply keep tightening the bandage until the bleeding stops! Application of this versatile bandage is demonstrated in MTLE training materials.

The TRIK also contains a versatile and highly absorbent gauze dressing, commonly referred to as an abdominal bandage (ABD) pad. The ABD pad can be used with medical tape in the TRIK to treat and cover smaller wounds or as packing material for deeper wounds.

Carry your TRIK on your person at all times! Whether it is a TRIK or any other first-aid/trauma care kit, it will do you no good unless you have it with you.

Remember, no one should die from extremity bleeding! It's that simple. The interventions discussed for bleeding control start with having ready access to the essential tools contained in the TRIK.

What do you do if for some reason you encounter a life-threatening situation but don't have a TRIK on hand? You improvise! With an understanding of how the various bleeding interventions discussed work, you now have the knowledge to make a wound dressing from almost anything.

> "If you carry a knife, the world is your bandage!"

Why is there not a tourniquet—separate from the Israeli Battle Dressing that features a tourniquet function—included in the TRIK?

And why is there no hemostatic agent included in the TRIK? In a perfect world, every officer would also carry these items. However, getting an officer to carry even one treatment option at all times is difficult enough. Getting officers to carry all of the treatment options is practically impossible. The TRIK contains the widest range of portable bleeding treatment options at an affordable price.

Once you have gained control over a life-threatening bleed, the next step is to focus on securing the victim's airway, applying a set of very quick and simple maneuvers. As noted earlier, keep in mind that less than 1 percent of U.S. soldiers die from airway obstruction in combat, according to the Wound Data and Munitions Effectiveness Team (1970). So the chances that an intervention is needed are small. However, you should know how to assess and intervene, if necessary. How do you go about quickly assessing whether the victim's airway is open?

Start with determining whether the victim is able to speak by asking him to respond to a simple question, such as "What is your name?", or "Can you tell me if you are O.K?" *Always the first step,* the verbal response test is useable at any distance.

If yes, the victim is able to respond to you, it means his airway is open and he is able to breathe. The victim's ability to speak means no intervention is necessary and you can proceed to the next step in treating the victim.

If on the other hand, the victim is not verbally responsive, you will need to determine if he is still alive. How can you tell? If you are close, determine if you can see, hear, or feel him breathing. If you are at a distance, look to see if the victim's chest rises and falls with each inhalation and exhalation of the breath.

If yes, the victim is still alive and breathing. Protect his airway by gently tilting the head back and lifting the chin up. If, however, there is a possibility of blunt force trauma due to a hit with a blunt object, a fall, or collision, then we must assume that the individual has sustained a cervical spine, or neck, injury.

To protect the neck and help prevent against any possible further injury, the "jaw-thrust maneuver" is preferable to tilting the head back and lifting the chin up. The jaw-thrust maneuver is performed with the victim reclining on his back with the face up. The rescuer positions himself at the crown of the victim's head, places his thumbs on the victim's cheekbones and the four fingers of both of his hands along each side of the victim's mandible, or lower jawbone. The rescuer then opens the victim's airway by gently thrusting, or tilting, the lower jawbone upward while keeping the neck and head stable.

Once the victim's airway is opened, you can then insert a nasopharyngeal airway (NPA), which is a relatively thin and gently angled tube, in through one nostril of the victim's nose and down into the nasopharynx, the upper end of the throat, to keep his airway open. NPAs are also commonly known as trumpets due to the flared-end design at one end of the tube. Note that an NPA must be well lubricated to prevent injury to the nasal passage upon insertion.

An NPA is also among the essential tools contained within the TRIK! But to be clear, the goal of using an NPA is to keep a semiconscious or completely unconscious victim's airway open—not to be confused with making a non-breathing victim breathe! Once you secure the victim's breathing ability, you can then focus on expediting his extraction to the safe zone where he can be transported for treatment at the nearest hospital.

Are there any contraindications for using an NPA? Yes, there are instances in which you should *NOT* use an NPA, such as: on a fully alert and aware individual who is breathing; if the victim does not tolerate the NPA and you encounter resistance upon attempting to insert the NPA, such as gag reflex or the victim resists and tries to self-extract the device; or there is severe facial trauma and you simply cannot find the nasal passage to insert the NPA. Additionally, you should *NOT* use an NPA on a small or prepubescent child with a narrower, shorter airway opening than the NPA can accommodate due to the risk of causing further injury. In this case, the NPA must be sized appropriately.

When used in appropriate circumstances, the NPA poses minimal risk to the victim. The benefit outweighs the risk, as an NPA can serve to keep the airway of a semiconscious or unconscious victim open so he can continue to effectively breathe when moved, carried, or dragged to safety.

What if you determine that a victim is both unresponsive and clearly no longer breathing upon closer examination? You discontinue rescue efforts and proceed to the next priority.

But what about attempting to perform cardio pulmonary resuscitation (CPR) as a life-saving measure? You cannot afford the risk of performing CPR in the street when the active threat of an offender persists.

Performing CRP in the street removes at least one officer, or sometimes even two, from the fight. Moreover, CPR loses all effectiveness, if interrupted because an officer has to fight off a threat. Therefore, it cannot be overemphasized that the best treatment for a non-breathing person is threat elimination! Removing the threat from the situation expedites access to comprehensive care for a victim in critical condition and protects others from injury.

Another potential complication that a first responder may encounter is an *open pneumothorax,* or hole in the chest, as a result of a penetrating injury. The term *pneumothorax* breaks down simply as "pneumo" meaning air and "thorax" meaning chest.

A pneumothorax is divided into two general types: *open* and *closed.* Air can only enter the chest from one of two sources. There must be either a hole in the chest wall or a hole in the lung.

Within the scope of this book, we will focus on the *open* pneumothorax. This type of pneumothorax occurs with a large injury to the chest wall which leaves a hole larger than one's finger. How does an open pneumothorax compromise a victim's breathing ability? Air enters through the hole in the victim's chest cavity, causing the lung to collapse. When an individual suffers a penetrating injury to the chest, be it from a gunshot wound, knife, or other object, the risks remain the same: blood leaking into the chest and air filling up the chest and becoming trapped.

There is not much we can do in the street relative to addressing the first risk of bleeding into the chest, because we cannot simply reach in and apply direct pressure where it is needed. For these cases, we must rely on indirect counter measures, such as keeping the patient warm and treating for presumed shock.

The other risk associated with penetration of the chest involves the accumulation of air inside the chest cavity but outside the lung. Looking back at the Wound Data and Munitions Effectiveness Team data, we know that only 1 to 4 percent of soldiers die from a pneumothorax, so the risk is actually relatively low. Nevertheless, it is worth discussing.

An isolated hole in the lung more often occurs from blunt force trauma when the lung "pops" like a balloon and then releases air into the chest cavity. When this happens, air escapes the lung but cannot go back in, therefore accumulating in the chest. As air accumulates with each breath, it begins to build up pressure within the chest.

The build-up of pressure in the chest can compromise the function of the heart and impede blood flow returning from the lower body back to the heart. The end result can be death. This escalating, life-threatening condition is known as a *tension pneumothorax* and is presumed to occur on a rarer basis. Fortunately for law enforcement officers, we wear body armor that protects the chest and thus should offer some protection from blunt force chest trauma.

A gunshot or knife stabbing that penetrates the chest wall and pierces the lung can also cause a tension pneumothorax. When this condition occurs, the hole in the chest frequently seals up quickly due to the surrounding skin and soft tissues. Thus, only a hole is left in the lung, which may continue to leak air and thus cause a pressure situation in the chest as described previously.

The simple fix for a tension pneumothorax is to place a needle into the chest and relieve the pressure. The technique, however, is somewhat invasive and therefore beyond the scope of this book.

The good thing about an open pneumothorax is that it is rarely a life-threatening situation. As one breathes in, air is sucked into the chest through the wound hole as well as through the nose and mouth. Thus, an open pneumothorax is also known simply as a "sucking chest wound."

Pressure does not accumulate in the chest with an open pneumothorax. Because the hole exists communicably with the atmosphere, it allows for constant air decompression.

In these cases, however, the lung will typically collapse and cease to refill with air with each breathe. Since most people can breathe with only one lung, this rarely presents a major issue in the street. Needless to say, a hole in one's chest is disturbing, especially when it spurts blood, air, and bubbles.

The way we generally treat an open pneumothorax is by simply covering the hole to the chest. The only caveat is that we do not want to completely seal off the hole, as we need to allow for the release of the air leaking from the lung into the chest. The air must continue to be able to effectively escape from the chest; otherwise, the risk may escalate to life-threatening consequences of a pressure-building, or tension, pneumothorax.

In the case of an open pneumothorax, we can use a plastic or foil dressing. From the TRIK, we can use the outer green foil bag as a dressing. We lay the foil dressing over the hole and secure it to the outside of the chest wall using tape. However, we only secure three of the four sides with tape to provide an air escape valve through one side. When the victim inhales, the foil will suck down onto the chest. When he exhales, it will relax. If pressure builds up in the chest, the valve will release, and the air will escape.

The key take-away point here is that you should treat *ALL* penetrating chest injuries as if they were open pneumothoraxes. Understand that while there are many different types of pneumothoraxes, it is not your job as an officer to diagnose which type a victim may have. The important thing to remember is that all types of pneumothoraxes can produce fatal consequences.

Once you have treated a victim's life-threatening bleeding injuries and secured his airway and ability to breathe, the next step is to prevent him from succumbing to shock.

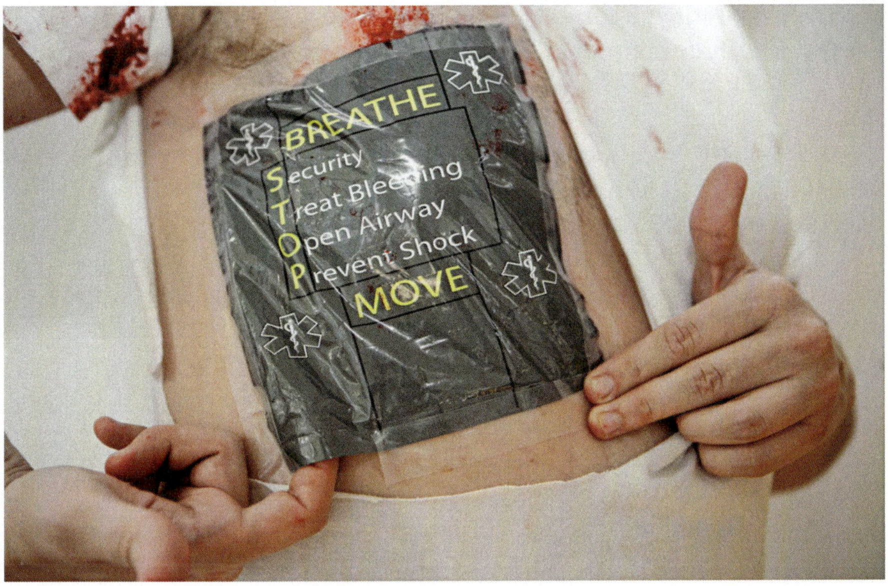

Three-sided dressing.

What is shock exactly? Shock is the body's inability to deliver oxygen to its tissues. When an injury produces significant blood loss, the blood supply to the vital organs becomes deficient, and the consequences can be fatal.

How do you know when to treat a victim for shock? The victim may present as pale, sweaty, shivering, agitated, or confused. You can assess the victim for mentation, or his ability to think clearly, by attempting to gather some intelligence from him. For instance, ask the victim his name, where he is, and what happened. When the victim responds, assess whether he is making any sense.

If yes, he is making sense, treat him for shock and move on to the next step.

If no, he is not making much, if any, sense, then also treat him for shock.

Anyone semiconscious or unconscious should be considered to be in a state of shock. Bottom line: *Always* treat for shock because of the potentially fatal risk! It can't hurt!

How do you treat a victim for shock? First, secure both your weapon and his weapon! The victim may be confused, agitated, and scared and try to grab his or your weapon. You can then elevate the victim's legs to help the blood flow back upstream toward the heart and brain. An easy way to remember this step is "face pale, raise tail."

Next, wrap the victim to keep him warm, preferably using the emergency blanket contained in the TRIK. Otherwise, you can use a jacket or any other article of clothing or fabric on hand that will suffice. Note that it is most essential to wrap the victim's head and torso. However, the more of his body you can wrap, the better! If possible, consider the immediate evacuation of the victim to safety for transportation to the nearest hospital or trauma center for further treatment.

Understandably, some life-threatening situations will not allow you the chance to wrap a victim for warmth or elevate his legs to improve upstream blood flow. What do you do then? Continue to reassess the victim for airway compromise and extract with haste.

What's the importance of keeping the victim warm in helping to prevent shock? Warmth helps to maintain the blood's ability to clot, improving long-term outcomes for victims suffering from blood loss.

When an individual suffers significant blood loss, many tissues throughout the body become starved of oxygen, as blood is the carrier of oxygen. Cells need oxygen to live. When they are oxygen-starved, they can continue to function on a temporary basis but, in doing so, they produce lactic acid. An accumulation of lactic acid disturbs the overall pH balance of the body, making it overly acidic. For a limited amount of time, your body can "buffer" itself to maintain a normal pH of around 7.34. After that time, the body's pH will then begin to turn increasingly acidic. When this happens, many body functions, the blood's clotting ability being one of them, begin to fail because they are pH sensitive.

In other words, warmth helps prevent what is known as the "lethal triad." The more a victim bleeds, the more acidic his blood becomes due to a lack of oxygen. The more acidic the blood becomes, the colder the victim gets. The colder he gets, the more he bleeds. Why?

Blood does not form clots below 93° Fahrenheit, producing a dangerous effect. In essence, cold kills! Again, the need to *always* treat for shock can't be overemphasized. Maintaining warmth is absolutely crucial to enabling effective bleeding control.

Let's take a look at how to assess the seriousness of a victim's shock potential due to blood loss. What does life-threatening blood loss *really* look like?

To help illustrate, consider that the amount of blood in an average-size, adult human body equates to approximately five one-liter bottles of soda. How many liters of blood the human body can afford to lose ultimately depends on an individual's weight and height.

Have you ever spilled an entire liter bottle of soda on the ground? Even just one bottle makes for a very large spill, right? Yet for an average size adult, losing the equivalent of a one-liter bottle of blood

What life-threatening blood loss looks like.

would be considered reversible shock. The human body has an impressive blood reserve in the event of loss due to injury. The body can continue to function with minimal consequence.

Have you ever given blood? If not, you should. Whenever you donate blood, you effectively give half a liter each time.

So what does severe shock look like in terms of blood loss? A loss of three to four liters of blood, or approximately a three-foot diameter pool of blood, generally equates to severe shock. With this amount of blood loss, the victim will require a blood transfusion to replace the loss, along with fluids to preserve bodily function and blood pressure.

At a loss of five liters of blood, or approximately a four-to-five-foot pool of blood, it's game over! Note, however, that blood lost doesn't only end up on the floor.

Do not rely solely on the amount of pooled blood on the floor as an assessment tool. Just because you can't see the blood on the floor, doesn't mean it's not lost.

Where else can that much blood possibly go besides the floor? The blood can also leak into the chest, abdomen, pelvis, and retroperitoneum, which is the space behind the abdominal cavity.

In assessing the amount of blood loss, keep in mind that the victim's clothing can absorb a fair amount of blood as well. Darker colored clothes, such as a black or navy blue police uniform, can make it hard to see bloodstains. Be diligent when assessing a victim for blood loss and always expose all injuries so you can get a more accurate picture of how serious his condition is. The TRIK includes a pair of shears for just this purpose. After you expose the victim's injuries, take care to then quickly cover him to prevent heat loss.

Many injuries can cause internal bleeding which cannot be effectively treated in the street at any level of care. Therefore, to improve an injured victim's chances for survival, focus on taking cover and eliminating any active threat so you can then treat the victim for shock and help to evacuate him from the scene to obtain comprehensive trauma care.

In effect, the best medical intervention in the street is to apply the best tactical option. Threat elimination is always the top priority as it speeds the victim's access to comprehensive care.

Once you have gained control over any active threats and treated any life-threatening injuries, it's time to *MOVE!* The goal is to get off of the target and stay alive and in the fight!

For the first stage of movement, assess whether you can move and whether the injured victim you are assisting can also move. Determine if you and the victim can both move on your own or whether an assisted extraction is required. Even if you cannot change your position, try moving your body to assess functional ability. Move your hands and fingers to evaluate limitations.

Next, for the second stage of movement, consider your options for transport to comprehensive emergency care. Determine which mode of transport—an ambulance or a squad car—is most accessible. An ambulance is clearly the best form of transportation, as the workspace is maximized. A police vehicle is rarely a good choice. But if time is ticking away, the most accessible ride is going to be the best option.

Interestingly, a study performed in Los Angeles during the 90s, titled *Emergency Medical Services (EMS) vs Non-EMS Transport of Critically Injured Patients,* revealed lower mortality rates among injured victims transported by civilian means versus ambulances. Published in the *The JAMA Network Archives of Surgery,* the study revealed that the ambulance crews spent too much time on the scene (Cornwell, Belzberg, Hennigan, Maxson, Montoya, Rosenbluth, Velmahos, Berne, and Demetriades, 2000).

At that time, emergency medical services applied measures at the scene to enhance survival of cardiac patients but unknowingly increased the mortality of trauma patients. Current standards strive to minimize the amount of time spent treating trauma patients at the scene by stabilizing them as quickly as possible and then transporting for more comprehensive treatment at an emergency care facility.

Do you know what the "golden hour" is relative to a seriously injured victim's chances for survival? The golden hour is the maximum amount of allowable time between the occurrence of the injury and access to comprehensive emergency care. As the elapsed time between injury and care exceeds the golden hour, mortality rates increase considerably.

In general, an ambulance is the preferred method of transport, although exceptions may apply depending on the particular circumstances of a situation.

For example, say your partner is injured near your squad car and the nearest hospital is just seven blocks away—in that case, a squad car may well be your best bet. On the other hand, if your partner is injured on the second floor of a building and the nearest hospital is seven miles away, then an ambulance is more than likely your best bet. In any case, determine the best method of transport before initiating the evacuation process. Whenever possible, always have an evacuation plan in your head: Where am I going, and how am I getting there?

To summarize, let's review the Medical Tactics for Law Enforcement (MTLE) life-saving script: BREATHE, S-T-O-P, MOVE!

BREATHE: Before you do anything, breathe to compose yourself and gain control over both your body and mind to help mitigate any fear. This step applies to both you and any injured victims you are assisting. If necessary, avoid looking at an injury until you have gained enough composure to effectively deal with the situation. Remember, emotion and perception can influence performance, and performing the dynamic breathing technique can help you gain control over both.

S-T-O-P: **S**ecure the situation, **T**reat bleeding, **O**pen airway, and **P**revent shock.

- *Secure the situation:* Perform a quick **S-C-A-N.** **S**urveil area for threats, **C**ontrol variables, **A**ssess goals, and **N**ever take your eyes off the threat! Situational awareness is vital to planning and implementing an appropriate response!
- *Treat bleeding:* Remember to apply strategic tactics before treatment! Then treat any active significant bleeding while minimizing further exposure to any threats. Until the victim is under cover or concealment, it is best to defer any treatment. Treat only

what MUST be treated, such as immediate life-threatening loss of blood.

- *Open Airway:* Assess an injured victim's ability to verbally respond. If the victim can speak, then skip to the next step. If the victim is marginally or completely verbally unresponsive but is still breathing, then consider using a nasal pharyngeal airway to protect and stabilize his airway. If you are injured but able to speak, then vocalize to your partner and other fellow officers your condition, if possible. Remember, if you are breathing, and able to think and speak, then you are *NOT* dead! You are still in the fight!
- *Prevent Shock:* Regardless of the victim's degree of injury and blood loss, always treat for shock. Secure all weapons, assess whether the victim is making any sense, elevate legs to improve upstream blood flow back to the heart and brain, and provide warmth to prevent the risk of hypothermia.

MOVE: If you have not already moved to cover or concealment, do so. Then determine best method of transport—ambulance or squad car—and help extract the victim from the scene so he may obtain comprehensive emergency care.

Let's quickly test out your knowledge of how to apply the lifesaving MTLE script. Say you sustain a large wound to the back? You are bleeding as a result of the injury although not significantly.

Is the injury life threatening? No, since the blood loss is not significant, the injury is not life threatening. You are still breathing and able to think and speak clearly.

So what do you do to treat the wound? Before you act, take a critical timeout to breathe and gain your composure over the situation. Remember, tactics before treatment! Take cover and eliminate any active threat first. Then treat yourself by applying direct pressure, pressing the shoulder wound against a wall or floor to help minimize the bleeding. Bandage the wound when convenient and evacuate yourself as soon as possible to safety for emergency care. It's that simple.

Remember, you have the ability to gain and maintain control over your physical and psychological response to a life-threatening situation. Some pearls of wisdom to prevail by include: take that critical timeout to BREATHE, disrupt your fear-based response and tunnel vision, and pull yourself together. Never rush into a situation. Always S-T-O-P and determine your tactical plan before intervening and then MOVE to safety when possible.

Also, keep it simple. Remember limited input about a situation facilitates better decision making under pressure.

Up to this point, the focus has been on developing your fundamental understanding of the MTLE training assessment and intervention steps for balancing medical life-saving and mission priorities in the street to increase the odds of favorable outcomes. In the next chapter, we will delve deeper into *Movement*.

CHAPTER 5

MOVEMENT

STRATEGIC APPROACHES AND ESCAPE TACTICS FOR MAKING IT OUT OF THE HOT ZONE ALIVE

Most law enforcement officers receive various types of training during the course of their career. But, have you and your colleagues ever been specifically trained on different types of rescue methods, such as assists, drags, and carries?

If you are like most of the law enforcement officers I have met and trained, the answer is probably *not* or *very little,* if any. Yet, it is absolutely imperative that you develop your knowledge base and skills for *when* to apply and *how* to effectively perform different rescue methods to survive and prevail out in the street. In this chapter, I will explain the value of this special training and introduce you to the various assist, drag, and carry rescue methods as taught in the MTLE training program.

For starters, I can't overemphasize enough the importance of appropriately applying and performing rescue maneuvers to make it out of the hot zone alive. Why? Because chances are that emergency medical services cannot reach you or other injured victims in the hot zone until the imminent threat has been neutralized.

With that being the case, what is the key determining factor in planning a successful rescue? The key determinant is *risk assessment,* which essentially comes down to effectively applying this very basic rule: *Risk a lot to save a lot, and risk a little save a little.*

In other words, you must weigh the benefits against the risks in determining your response. The ability to think clearly in weighing the risks and benefits of a situation and to decide and act quickly under duress largely depends on training and practice.

Remember the study led by Dr. Sztajnkrycer of the Mayo Clinic (2010) as referenced in Chapter 1? The police officers in the study responded differently in the field than in the classroom setting due to a lack of essential education and practical training. In every scenario, the officers acted based on their emotions rather than tactics, rushing in to save a fallen officer and putting themselves at risk in the process.

What are the consequences when emotions dominate tactics in the street? The potential for incurring more injuries generally increases significantly, as officers take action based on emotion. If officers sustain injuries, then their ability to respond to the threat and perform rescues is compromised, resulting in the worst possible outcome. Thus, the importance of appropriate assessment before taking action cannot be overemphasized.

What are the most common pitfalls in risk assessment? Although good-intentioned, the duty-bound police officer mindset is a common pitfall. Officers are innately compelled by the duty to act, meaning "doing something is better than doing nothing." Resorting to poor tactics, however, can get you and others killed!

If the assessed risks of an action outweigh the rewards, "doing nothing is better than doing something." Therefore, when taking action is necessary, you must succeed!

Other typical risk assessment pitfalls include the natural, fear-based human response, lack of practical training and conditioning, inability to determine the situational scope, and underestimation of tasks required to prevail. In effect, officers end up letting their emotions and instincts dictate their decisions and actions rather than tactics.

Many injuries are unable to be treated in the street. Therefore, threat elimination is key to enabling emergency medical services access to the scene to help stabilize and transport injured victims as soon as possible. Or, if you cannot readily evacuate a victim to receive comprehensive care, even a partial rescue to a safer zone can offer the chance to help stabilize his condition in the interim.

Fundamentally, tactical training and conditioning through regular practice is all that stands between an officer and an instinct-driven response. Yet, many officers have little, if any, formal training or practice in strategic approaches and escape tactics for making it out of the hot zone alive. As a result, officers frequently encounter tremendous difficulties while performing instinctive rescues in the absence of such tactical training.

The lack of a script for responding to a campus shooting, for instance, or other highly volatile situation, frequently results in an ineffective use of officers on the scene. Relying on instinct, in the absence of essential tactical training, officers operating under extreme duress are apt to focus on victim rescue as opposed to focusing on threat elimination as the top priority. Until the threat is eliminated or brought under control, however, emergency medical services cannot gain access to the scene to stabilize and transport victims to a comprehensive care facility.

A simulated scenario we commonly practice for in the MTLE training involves a responding officer rolling up on a police vehicle. The responding officer stops approximately twenty yards away, as he notices two victims in proximity to the police vehicle he just rolled up on. From a distance, the officer sees that one of the victims is a police officer, and he is not moving, appearing to be mortally wounded. The second victim screams for assistance, stating she is bleeding.

At this point, the responding officer does not know whether the female subject is actually a victim, as she claims, or the offender. Nor does the officer know if another threat lurks close. At this point, the officer has a critical decision to make: He can hold at a distance, continue to assess the situation, and wait for assistance before making a move toward the vehicle; or, he can rapidly launch into action and go to the aid of the downed officer and also try to rescue or address the unknown female subject.

If the female subject is persuasive and the responding officer lets emotion and perceived urgency dominate his reaction, he risks becoming a victim himself. Remember, it is still unconfirmed at this point whether the female subject is truly a victim or an armed offender. This is where an officer's mental preparedness is absolutely vital in effectively determining his reaction to a situation—a tactical mindset must *always* prevail!

Frequently, officers let their guard down and do not consider all the possibilities, especially if the perceived victim is very convincing and there is an emotional attachment to the downed officer. In MTLE taining we have tested this scenario on more than one hundred law enforcement officers and agents and, interestingly, this error in judgment is not uncommon. We also observed, among more than 50 percent of the officers tested, that they failed to find a concealed weapon on the female subject in question.

In an ideal world, in which a tactical mindset prevails, this scenario should unfold as follows:

- The responding officer rolls up on the scene and initially keeps his distance. He remotely assesses the situation by actively looking for any remaining threats.
- The responding officer then looks to see if there are any signs of life or movement from the downed officer. This includes trying to assess the downed officer's condition through the use of verbal commands and questions. From this assessment, the responding officer should realize that the downed officer is dead, and therefore no urgency exists to perform a rescue at this time.
- Next, the responding officer should direct his attention to the female subject in question. He should assume that, despite her screams for help, she is still a potential offender, an unknown, and should be treated as such.
- The responding officer should engage in communication with the female subject by first asking her questions that pertain to her well-being, the context of the situation, and how it occurred. From this communication exchange and from her responses, the

officer may glean some tactical information about any other possible threats and other valuable information concerning the situation.

With this information, the responding officer is able to determine that performing a rescue for the female subject is not of an urgent need and that there is time to fortify his position and wait for backup assistance. By knowing the female subject is okay and that the downed officer is dead, no matter how emotionally taxing that may be, the responding officer can make the correct tactical decision based on data gathered rather than on emotion.

The absence of a tactical script also forces officers operating under intense pressure to make rash and often poor decisions about the types of assists, drags, or carries to perform in rescuing victims. For instance, in some situations carries may be inappropriately performed for victims that are capable of walking on their own or with minimal assistance, resulting in an ineffective use of officers on the scene.

What can we learn from actual situations, like campus shootings, for instance, and from simulated training scenarios like the one just described? Police officers can better prepare to respond to such potentially volatile situations in the future by training and practicing based on a tactical script designed to help quickly assess situational risks and respond appropriately.

The MTLE training program teaches officers a pre-scripted tactical response that can be adapted to various life-threatening situations out in the street. The program includes education and simulated training scenarios on the various types of assist, drag, and carry rescues that may be performed and how to effectively and expeditiously perform the rescues.

The training helps officers determine when an individual needs to be assisted, dragged, or carried to safety based on the situational factors. Key determinants include, for instance, the type and degree of injuries sustained, number of officers available to help, escape route terrain and distance, and the need to defend against further possible contact from any remaining threats.

Choosing the appropriate response helps to reduce further risk of injury and makes more effective use of the officers involved. The appropriate response can also save precious time, when every second counts and can mean the difference between life and death. Poor technique can hinder the rescue and even cause further injury to victims and rescuers.

For example, assisting officers' may leave themselves exposed and end up having to suddenly drop a victim on the ground during the rescue effort to react to contact from an offender. Or, poor handling of the victim could restrict his airway or cause dislocation or injury to his neck, shoulders, back, or limbs. Moreover, poor technique can limit the abilities of assisting officers to cover the distance and navigate difficult terrain or obstacles, such as stairways and doorways, to reach the safe zone.

Determining which rescue method to use begins with appropriate assessment of the situation and knowing which methods generally work best in which types of situations. For instance, certain methods are better suited to particular terrains or may make it easier to respond to contact from an offender.

The ability to effectively perform the different types of rescues depends on training and practice. Training to perform rescues is no different than training to perform other types of tactical maneuvers in the street. In other words, "train to rescue just like you train to fight!" Training and practice conditions you to anticipate difficulties and maintain better control over the mental and physical reactions produced with the natural human stress response. It is no coincidence that the fire service trains in performing rescues regularly. Rescue skills are perishables, and there is always room for improvement.

Assists, drags, and carries are perishable skills—"if you don't use it, you lose it." Performing the different types of rescues requires carefully coordinated movement. For instance, you may need to simultaneously address various issues of injured victims, such as keeping the airway open to preserve the ability to breathe and to prevent vomit aspiration and further damage to any broken bones. Sometimes, victims may panic, struggle, or even become combative and resist help because they are unable to think rationally due to shock or intense pain and fear of injuries sustained.

One of the most important skills to train for when it comes to rescues is performing the situation assessment, or "looking before you leap into action." The importance of situation assessment cannot be overstated, as it can mean the difference between life and death.

Appropriately performing assists, drags, or carries is secondary in importance to situation assessment. You will succeed, or fail, based on your ability to effectively assess the situation and plan an appropriate rescue.

How can you go about assessing the situation and determining a rescue response? By applying the tactical approach of the MTLE S-C-A-N script introduced earlier: S-urveil area, C-ontrol variables, A-ssess goals and N-ever lose sight of the threat!

But before beginning the MTLE SCAN maneuver, remember to take that critical timeout to just BREATHE! Take those few, but vital seconds to quickly gain control over your mental and physical reactions of your natural stress response to the situation at hand before proceeding based on the SCAN script.

Step 1: Surveil area. After you have gained your composure, the first step is to identify any remaining threats and injured victims. Are there still looming threats, or have they been brought under control? Are the injured victims on the scene still alive, or are they dead? If they are still alive, is a rescue needed or can they move to safety on their own? Are any of the victims actually offenders?

From a distance, it is more difficult to tell whether a victim is alive or has suffered a fatal injury. Remember that you can perform the *remote victim assessment* technique introduced earlier. Ask the victim to verbally respond to a simple question to confirm that his airway is open and he is still breathing.

If the victim is able to communicate verbally, then you can also assess his mental status. Are his responses logical? If he is not making much sense and his condition appears to be deteriorating, then he may be slipping into shock. Remember, one of the first signs of shock is confusion. This indicates that the brain is starved for oxygen and thus not working appropriately.

Suppose that the victim cannot respond verbally? You then determine if you can see the rise and fall of his chest to confirm breathing. Note that it may be more difficult to confirm breathing of an injured officer wearing body armor and other gear. Look for any signs of spontaneous movement.

Binoculars can aid your ability to perform remote victim assessment. Place binoculars on a level surface, if possible, and aim at the victim's chest to observe.

As you observe a victim's condition, notice whether he is bleeding at all. You can use the blood pool estimation technique introduced earlier. Remember that blood loss is not always readily visible on a victim who is wearing dark-colored clothing or bleeding internally. Also notice any visible disabilities, such as limbs that look broken or joints that look displaced. Lastly, notice if the victim is producing spontaneous movements.

If the victim is not breathing, then a rescue is unfortunately not indicated. Cardiopulmonary resuscitation is not performed in a dynamic tactical environment due to the exposure risk of contact from a looming threat and its overall limited effectiveness.

Rather, the best medicine for a non-breathing or other critically-wounded individual is to eliminate any remaining threats first to enable emergency medical services access to the scene. Swift transport of the victim to the nearest emergency department where he can receive comprehensive care is the only solution in this type of extreme situation.

Step 2: Control variables. The second step is focused on determining the severity of a victim's injuries and urgency of required treatment, and whether a rescue is necessary or self-extraction is possible, depending on the victim's ability to move. Once of you have determined the situational variables, consider what must be accomplished to address and manage the victim while moving him out of the hot zone to safety.

If the victim is unable to walk and you must perform a rescue, you will need to determine whether an assist, drag, or carry rescue will work best given the situational factors. To determine the best rescue method, you will also need to take into account the victim's physical size and limitations of injuries sustained, the number of officers available to assist in the rescue, and the distance and obstacles to navigate to reach safety.

As you consider all the various situational variables, don't forget the most significant variable YOU must control—your risk of exposure to a still looming threat! You must maintain your cover and ability to respond to contact, if necessary. If you become a victim too, then it's mission over! To maintain control over the situational variables, you must *weigh* and *manage* the risks versus the benefits before determining your course of action.

If you cannot readily assist an injured victim due to risk of exposure to contact, consider if he can self-treat his injuries in the meantime. Can you throw the necessary medical gear from where you are over to him?

For instance, can you throw over a Trauma Rapid Intervention Kit (TRIK)? If the victim is conscious and able to self-treat using the tools contained in the TRIK, it may be a much smarter and safer tactical solution in the interim than attempting to perform a rescue under a pending threat.

Step 3: Assess goals. The third step focuses on determining your goals for making it out of the hot zone alive. Once you have considered the various situational variables, determine the course of action to move yourself and the victims that need assistance from where you are to where you need to go to reach the safe zone. How will you get there? What do you need to do?

Plan the rescue mission, identifying the escape route and how you will navigate the terrain and any obstacles while maintaining your cover and ability to respond to contact along the route. Keep the end goal in mind, whether it's reaching emergency medical services at the scene, your own squad car, or even a civilian vehicle for transport to the nearest emergency department where comprehensive care can be provided.

The number of rescuers needed depends on the victim's physical size and the limitations of his injuries, as well as the distance and obstacles between where you are and where you need to go to reach safety. For example, fifteen to twenty rescuers are typically needed to carry one man two miles, according to Wilderness Medicine Recommendations (Forgey, 2006).

The potential for rescuer fatigue is a most essential planning consideration to keep in mind. Do you have the people and equipment you need to accomplish the rescue mission? Is your plan realistic and achievable?

Step 4: Never lose sight of the threat! This fourth, and last, step is the most crucial overall. As you execute your rescue mission, if at all possible DO NOT let your guard down for any amount of time—not even for a split second.

To make it out of the hot zone alive, you *must* make it your absolute top priority to stay on top of what the pending threats are and where they are at all times. Remember, a threat will seek to exploit any vulnerable point in your escape to take you out of the game. The threat could be a perceived victim.

Communicating your plan with the clearest and simplest instructions possible to other assisting officers and injured victims who are conscious can significantly increase the odds of successfully accomplishing the rescue mission. The assisting officers can better coordinate their rescue efforts, saving precious time and reducing the risks of further injury or exposure to contact. Victims made aware of your plan can better comply with any instructions with less risk of impeding the rescue efforts.

Whatever the situation you are facing, lead with a tactical approach, keep safe, and don't create more victims in the rescue process. Tactics must always prevail! You will inevitably encounter situations with unique or unusual circumstances in your line of duty as a law enforcement officer. Prepare to use the MTLE script as the basis for determining and executing your response while adapting to any unique circumstances as necessary. Be creative and resourceful in your training.

Rescuer safety is the No. 1 rule for emergency medical services. That rule applies to police officers out in the street as well, although it's a hard rule for officers to follow given their sense of duty. One must resist the urge to instinctively react to a situation based on a sense of duty and maintain a tactical mindset at all times. The only thing worse than one officer down, is two officers down.

Now that you have developed an overall understanding of how to apply the MTLE tactical approach, there are pros and cons to consider for each of the different types of rescue assist, drag, and carry methods. Your physical size and ability in conjunction with your training and practical experience in performing the different rescue maneuvers are among the important considerations for producing a successful outcome.

For example, do you have experience performing the maneuvers wearing your full uniform and gear versus plain civilian clothes without gear? Or, as a victim wearing little or no clothes? This is where realistic training is critical.

Wearing tactical gear tremendously affects your ability to grab and move another human. Clearly, wearing gear offers an officer the essential advantages of preparedness and protection. On the other hand, wearing gear can limit one's mobility to some degree and make many tasks more difficult.

You must develop your ability to carry out a rescue mission under the physical constraints of wearing YOUR gear. Otherwise, practicing without gear puts you at a significant disadvantage.

Also, consider whether you can enlist the help of other officers or civilians at the scene. What if there is no one around to assist in the rescue effort?

Say you must perform a carry; do you move the victim head or feet first? Can you manage the distance to the safe zone without succumbing to fatigue?

What about navigating difficult terrain, such as a hill, mud, or rocks? What about obstacles, such as doorways or stairs? What about points along the route that could leave you exposed and put you at risk for contact from the offender?

Addressing all of these considerations with expediency under intense pressure can seem very overwhelming, if not next to impossible. However, with training and practice gained in simulated real-life scenarios, you can develop your ability to swiftly and efficiently plan and execute the different rescue maneuvers. Training and practice are fundamental to successfully accomplishing a rescue mission.

Additionally, such experiments are crucial to exploiting one's own limitations and weaknesses. It is always better to go into a situation aware of one's limitations than to be surprised by them when lives are on the line.

When considering the various types of assist, drag, and carry rescue methods that may be utilized, keep in mind that size most certainly matters! Do not ignore the reality of your physical size and strength limitations or those of other assisting rescuers. Know your limits by training and regularly practicing the different rescue methods on individuals of different sizes and weights.

Let's review the pros and cons of the various rescue methods. First, let's take a look at three different options for *one-man rescues* in order of highly recommended, recommended, and not recommended.

Option 1 of 3: One-man, high-shoulder assist. This rescue method is highly recommended overall and is the first choice among one-man rescues. The method requires a relatively low level of training, setup, and application and is less physically demanding than performing the other one-man drag and carry methods described later, especially for a rescuer of smaller size and build.

High-shoulder assist.

One-man, high-shoulder assist:	Highly recommended overall		
Rating	Low	Moderate	High
Effectiveness			X
Training required	X		
Setup & application	X		
Speed			X
Accommodates terrain			X
Rescuer's ability to respond to environment			X
Physical demands	X		
Small rescuer capability			X

Moreover, the assist method offers the ability to move more quickly and accommodate longer distances, different types of terrain, and obstacles more easily compared to the other methods. Both the assisting officer and victim are also potentially able to defend against contact from a pending threat.

However, the one-man assist method requires a conscious victim and a partial ability to bear standing weight and walk on one leg! The injured limb should be positioned to the inside, alongside the assisting officer for support.

Option 2 of 3: One-man drag. This method, recommended overall, is the second choice among the one-man rescue methods. Compared to the one-man assist rescue method, the one-man drag method also requires relatively little training, setup, and application, although it is more physically demanding and harder to perform, particularly for a rescuer of smaller physical size and build. The method works fairly well for accommodating terrain while offering a high degree of effectiveness, speed of movement, and ability to respond to contact.

To rescue a fellow officer who is wearing either internal or external body armor with a vest carrier, the more effective approach is to drag him by the shoulder straps of his vest. Try to avoid using the drag or carry handles of a tactical vest, as they may have a tendency to tear or rip off during the rescue process. Alternatively, if the victim is not wearing a vest carrier, you can drag him by his belt.

If the victim is in plain civilian clothes, you might try dragging him by the top or collar of the back of his jacket or shirt, if the material is strong enough, or by his belt, if he happens to be wearing one. If he is

One-man drag

One-man drag:	Recommended overall		
Rating	Low	Moderate	High
Effectiveness			X
Training required	X		
Setup & application	X		
Speed			X
Accommodates terrain		X	
Rescuer's ability to respond to environment			X
Physical demands		X	
Small rescuer capability		X	

wearing little or no clothes, then you can drag him from under his armpits.

Also key is partially lifting the injured victim's head and upper torso up off of the ground when performing the drag. The less of the victim's body there is in contact with the ground, the less the drag resistance or friction created, making it easier on the assisting officer to move the victim. Another important consideration in using the drag method is keeping an unconscious victim's airway open so he can breathe.

Option 3 of 3: One-man, fireman's carry. This third, and last, one-man rescue method is NOT recommended overall! Even firemen today generally avoid using the fireman's carry, if at all possible, and so should officers in the street due to the significant risk of doing more harm than good.

The fireman's carry puts even larger and stronger rescuers under intense physical stress, often raising heart rates up to between 140 and 200 beats per minute! We tested this rescue method ourselves in the MTLE training program and scientifically with colleagues from

One-man, fireman's carry:	Not recommended overall		
Rating	**Low**	**Moderate**	**High**
Effectiveness			X
Training required			X
Setup & application		X	
Speed			X
Accommodates terrain		X	
Rescuer's ability to respond to environment	X		
Physical demands			X
Small rescuer capability	X		

Fireman's carry.

Wayne State University in Detroit, Michigan (Dennis and Bir, 2012). The method poses potentially serious and long-term, chronic back and shoulder injury risks to the rescuer. As the rescuer, you cannot afford risking injury to yourself, as it can take you out of the fight, or worse.

Incredibly few examples can be cited for when it would ever be appropriate to perform the fireman's carry rescue method anymore. The virtually obsolete method has been replaced by the aforementioned one-man drag rescue method.

Now, let's take a look at the three different options for *two-man rescues* that may be performed. The options are presented beginning with the most recommended option overall.

Option 1 of 3: Two-man, high-shoulder assist. Of the three different two-man rescue methods, this method is the most highly recommended overall. The two-man version of the high-shoulder assist method offers all of the same advantages of the one-man version with the added advantage of a second rescuer to distribute the injured victim's weight, making it easier to perform and all the more effective. Like its counterpart one-man version, the two-man version also requires a conscious victim with the partial ability to bear standing weight and walk on one leg.

Option 2 of 3: Two-man drag. This overall recommended method offers an effective rescue alternative when performing the two-man, high-shoulder assist is not possible. The two-man drag can be performed on an injured victim who is unconscious or cannot bear weight on either of his legs.

Two-man, high-shoulder assist:	Highly recommended overall		
Rating	Low	Moderate	High
Effectiveness			X
Training required	X		
Setup & application	X		
Speed			X
Accommodates terrain			X
Rescuer's ability to respond to environment			X
Physical demands	X		
Small rescuer capability			X

Two-man drag.

Two-man drag:	Recommended overall		
Rating	**Low**	**Moderate**	**High**
Effectiveness			X
Training required	X		
Setup & application	X		
Speed			X
Accommodates terrain		X	
Rescuer's ability to respond to environment			X
Physical demands		X	
Small rescuer capability			X

The two-man drag offers all of the same advantages as its one-man counterpart version with the added advantage of a second rescuer. Because the method distributes the injured victim's weight between two people, it lessens rescuer fatigue. Also, it's easier to perform a two-man versus and one-man drag over a longer distance, particularly for rescuers of smaller size and build. As with the one-man drag version, an important consideration is keeping an unconscious victim's airway open so he can breathe.

Two-man, forward-facing carry.

Two-man forward facing carry:	Recommended overall		
Rating	Low	Moderate	High
Effectiveness			X
Training required			X
Setup & application		X	
Speed			X
Accommodates terrain	X		
Rescuer's ability to respond to environment			X
Physical demands			X
Small rescuer capability		X	

Option 3 of 3: Two-man, forward-facing carry. This overall recommended method also offers an effective rescue alternative when performing either the preferred two-man, high-shoulder assist or two-man drag alternative are not possible. Like the two-man drag, the two-man carry can be performed on an injured victim who is unconscious or cannot bear standing weight or walk at all on either of his legs.

However, the two-man, forward-facing carry requires more training and setup and is more difficult to effectively perform compared to the two-man drag rescue method, especially for rescuers of smaller size and build. Again, another important consideration, as with both the two-man and one-man drag methods, is keeping an unconscious victim's airway open so he can breathe.

When it comes to the number of individuals available to assist in a rescue, a general rule of thumb is "three is better than two is better than one—and four is better yet!" Four is the ideal maximum number of rescuers for a single victim who is unconscious or unable to walk.

Three- or four-man, superman carry. This overall highly recommended rescue method further distributes the carry load among three or four rescuers. Thus, it offers the advantages of reduced fatigue over longer carry distances, increased speed of movement, and improved ability to manage an injured victim's airway. The two, front-carrying rescuers also have the ability to respond to contacts from a pending threat.

While the three- or four-man, superman carry also offers an improved ability to navigate difficult terrain, it tends to require a little more coordination for navigating certain obstacles, such as narrow doorways or stairways. Such obstacles are all manageable, but *only* if you train for them!

Are there other rescue options to consider beyond those discussed up to this point? Yes, the ones you devise!

Improvised carry. Sometimes the best carry rescue method combines what you have learned through tactical training and practical experience combined with your own creativity and resourcefulness. For example, you can consider using things found on the scene, such as a wheelchair in an office building, moving dolly or shopping cart in a

Three- or four-man, superman carry:	Highly recommended overall		
Rating	Low	Moderate	High
Effectiveness			X
Training required	X		
Setup & application	X		
Speed			X
Accommodates terrain			X
Rescuer's ability to respond to environment			X
Physical demands	X		
Small rescuer capability		X	

store or parking lot, or audio visual cart or table on wheels in a school classroom.

Or, you might try flipping over a rug or yanking down a thick curtain from a window in a room or public building entryway to facilitate carrying an injured victim to safety. You could even use a large, flat,

Superman carry.

Improvised carry:	Highly recommended overall		
Rating	**Low**	**Moderate**	**High**
Effectiveness			X
Training required	X		
Setup & application	X		
Speed			X
Accommodates terrain			X
Rescuer's ability to respond to environment			X
Physical demands	X		
Small rescuer capability			X

Rescue methods	Overall rating		
Type	**Not recommended**	**Recommended**	**Highly recommended**
One-man:			
One-man, high-shoulder assist			X
One-man drag		X	
One-man, fireman's carry	X		
Two-man:			
Two-man, high-shoulder assist			X
Two-man drag		X	
Two-man, forward-facing carry		X	
Three or four men:			
Three- or four-man, superman carry			X
Other:			
Improvised carry			X

and sturdy sheet of lumber or tarp as a makeshift stretcher, or a wheelbarrow lying around outdoors.

In summary, both the one-man and two-man, high-shoulder assists are considered highly recommended rescue methods overall for victims who are still conscious or have the partial ability to bear standing weight and walk using one of their legs. The three- or four-man, su-

Police squad car transfer.

perman carry and improvised carry rescue methods are also among the most highly recommended methods for use with victims who are either unconscious or unable to walk at all.

As for the remaining one-man and two-man drag and two-man, forward-facing carry rescue methods, they are all relatively effective and recommended as secondary alternatives for victims who are unconscious or unable to bear standing weight or walk at all. The one *exception* among all of the rescue methods presented is the fireman's carry, which is generally best avoided!

Performing an assist, drag, or carry rescue method to move an injured victim to the safe zone is only the first stage of movement. The next stage of movement involves evacuation of the victim to receive comprehensive care via emergency medical services transport or your own squad car or other mode of transport, such as a civilian vehicle.

Transferring a victim into your own squad car or other civilian vehicle may pose some challenges in terms of the size and weight of the injured victim, vehicle size and height, and number of rescuers available to assist. Thus, it's important to train and perform practice drills with just your squad car or other types of civilian vehicles in the event emergency medical services cannot make it in time to transport the victim to comprehensive care.

Your goal is to load the victim into the vehicle while simultaneously managing his airway and other injuries during the trip. You can use the victim's weight to your advantage, for instance, when loading him into a vehicle. If there is enough room, depending on the type and size of the vehicle, such as a larger sedan or an SUV, you can position one or two rescuers inside the backseat or back hatch area to help receive the victim.

Allow the victim to fall forward into the vehicle while a second rescuer pulls him from the inside. By using the momentum initiated by gravity and the victim's own weight, the rescuer can essentially control the fall of the victim into the vehicle.

Whether you will need to travel a few blocks or several miles to reach the nearest hospital, generally the safest bet is to load the victim inside the main passenger area of the vehicle. If you are going to travel a very short distance of one hundred feet or less, then you could potentially transport the victim on top of the vehicle or in the trunk. If you utilize this transport method, you must maintain a slow enough speed so the victim doesn't slide off the vehicle or move around in the trunk and incur further injury. Remember the opening sequence to the television series "MASH," in which the wounded are transported on the hoods of the jeeps?

When it comes to increasing your odds of successfully performing a rescue mission, whether it involves an assist, drag, or carry, the overall most important takeaway is: tactics must prevail! Train hard and practice often—just as if you are in a real fight for survival in the street.

Always train wearing your gear, otherwise you will operate at a major disadvantage in a real-life setting. Regularly practice the various assist, drag, and carry rescue methods to preserve your training knowledge; rescue skills are considered perishable.

Plan ahead for potential life-threatening street scenarios. Carry your Trauma Rapid Intervention Kit (TRIK) on your person and consider other essential equipment you may need to attach to your vest, using webbing or carabiners.

When you first arrive at the scene, remember to take that critical timeout and just BREATHE! Resist the urge to rush into the situation. You must maintain a tactical, goal-oriented mindset. If you rush into the situation without a strategic plan in mind, or panic, you jeopardize the safety of others, as well as your own.

Once you have gained your mental and physical composure while focusing on simply breathing, it's time to apply the tactical approach of the Medical Tactics for Law Enforcement (MTLE) S-C-A-N script:

S-urveil area, C-ontrol variables, A-ssess goals, and N-ever lose sight of the threat!

If others are available on the scene to assist you in performing the rescue, let them. Be prepared to adapt to the situation and think outside the box, if necessary. Exercise your creativity and resourcefulness, utilizing whatever objects you can find around you to facilitate the rescue effort. And always keep focused on the end goals: to *survive* and *prevail!*

CHAPTER 6

BUILDING ON TACTICAL LIFE-SAVING KNOWLEDGE WITH PRACTICAL TRAINING

Empower to Survive and Train to Prevail.

I established Medical Tactics with the express purpose of empowering law enforcement officers and other public safety specialists with the training and tools to *survive and prevail* in life-threatening situations encountered in the line of duty. And it is to this end that I designed the Medical Tactics for Law Enforcement (MTLE) training program and essential life-saving tools of the accompanying Trauma Rapid Intervention Kit (TRIK).

This book is not intended to replace the actual MTLE training. It is impossible to replace physical training through written word. One must experience the concepts audibly and visually in a tactical learning environment.

My purpose in producing this book was to introduce you to the core concepts of the MTLE training program: *mindset, mechanics, management,* and *movement.* The book up to this point has been dedicated to exploring these four concepts and the life-saving tools of the accompanying TRIK for treating traumatic injuries in the street.

This final chapter will emphasize the importance of training hard and practicing often—just as if you are in a fight for survival in the street. In other words, it's time to *get very real with your training* so you can survive and prevail in the face of real life-threatening danger. The MTLE training program and accompanying TRIK serve to help address *real* and serious deficiencies in current law enforcement first-responder, first-aid education, training, and tools.

The MTLE training program and TRIK address deficiencies identified through my own practical knowledge and experience gained working as a trauma surgeon and as a police officer as well as those shared by my colleagues in both worlds. The MTLE comprehensive trauma response system integrates what I've experienced and learned firsthand about the importance of maintaining a tactical mindset with what I know working as a trauma surgeon.

When trauma occurs in the street, your mind must quickly process the situational variables and then strategically determine the appropriate medical intervention to apply. *What do you do now? What are your options? How do you minimize further exposure to threats and risk of injury to yourself or others? Who do you treat first? What, where, when, and how do you apply medical treatment?*

Among the psychological concepts at play are perceptions and emotions. Both serve such a large role in influencing one's decisions

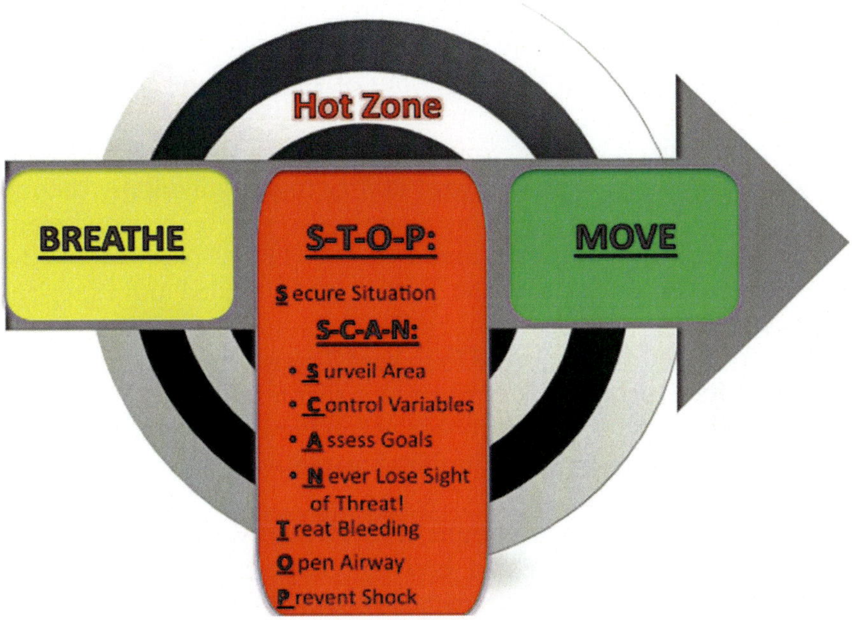

Medical Tactics for Law Enforcement.

and actions when responding to stresses that they must be given the proper credit.

The MTLE training program is designed to help empower you with a pre-scripted response to facilitate life-saving decision making under pressure, and the essential knowledge and tools to skillfully apply medical tactics to treat traumatic injuries that occur in the street. The easy-to-recall, BREATHE, STOP and SCAN, MOVE script provides a decision guide to help officers determine and deliver the appropriate responses in different life-threatening situations. The hands-on training teaches you how to effectively adapt and apply the MTLE script to respond to virtually any street situation.

The MTLE training program expands on the practical application of the four core concepts introduced in this book:

- *Mindset,* conditioning of the mind to help limit the negative effects of extreme stress and improve critical decision making in life-threatening situations;
- *Mechanics,* understanding the fundamentals of injury and separating medical fact from fiction;

- *Management,* recognizing and understanding when and how to treat life-threatening injuries; and
- *Movement,* effectively planning and safely performing assists, carries, and drags to make it out of the hot zone alive.

As emphasized earlier, your knowledge of these core life-saving concepts is only as useful as your ability to actually apply them in a real-life street situation. Effective application of the various medical tactics using the tools contained in the TRIK requires hands-on training and practice under the guidance of a skilled and experienced instructor.

Reality-based training (RBT) is key! The MTLE program consists of an eight-hour, didactic and practical intensive training. The dynamic training experience teaches the fundamentals of how to survive traumatic injury and prevail in life-threatening street situations as introduced in this book.

Since perception is paramount, as a student you can expect to take away a new understanding of how to recognize and effectively treat traumatic injuries under extremely stressful conditions. You will learn what is a lethal wound and what is not, when to treat and when not to, and how to effectively apply medical tactics to manage such injuries until help can reach you. In effect, you will get a crash course in ten-minute medicine.

The training course integrates lecture with interactive learning aids and simulated learning scenarios. Students are provided with opportunities to practice responding to various simulated, stress-filled street scenarios. In specific, you will learn how to maintain a tactical mindset under pressure and apply the various medical tactics introduced in this book—from bleeding control, airway management, and shock prevention to appropriate rescue assists, drags, and carries.

Students of the MTLE course receive an in-depth instruction manual consisting of more than 160 pages with color illustrations. Designed for use as an interactive learning aid, the manual details the tactical training techniques presented in the course, including simple and easy-to-recall mnemonic devices and step-by-step application instructions.

A summary of the key concepts introduced here, and to be explored in greater depth through the training course, is provided for your reference in the *Appendix* section of this book. Comprehensive videos and learning tools exist online, as well as access to the instructors for questions.

In addition to the course training manual, students receive take-home tools which include a TRIK. Upon completing the course, students take with them all of the training materials and tools used so they may continue practicing their new tactical life-saving skills and help train fellow officers.

Emergency medical services (EMS) students who complete the MTLE course may also earn accredited continuous education (CE) hours. EMS professionals interested in earning CE credits should let the Medical Tactics training staff know when registering to the take the course.

Through the MTLE training experience and following a plan for continued, regular practice, you can effectively help avoid the potential negative consequences of succumbing to the human stress response, your own worst enemy.

Your perception, fear, mindset, and physiology all culminate in producing your overall response to a situation. Therefore, when the stress response takes over, you run the risk of panicking under pressure and making decisions and taking action based on raw survival instincts rather than mission-minded, strategic tactics.

Through the simulated street experiences offered through the MTLE training program and continuous post-training practice, you can effectively condition your mind and body to improve your response in a variety of different high-stress, life-threatening situations. Combining a fundamental education of anatomy and physiology with practical training experiences will enable you to make better informed decisions and deliver a more predictable, favorable response.

After all, stalking danger comes with your duty as a police officer to serve and protect the public and greater good. You must therefore be prepared with the medical life-saving knowledge, training, and tools to effectively treat yourself or others, if injured in the street, until help can reach you.

My greatest hope is that by empowering our law enforcement officers and public safety specialists with the tactical life-saving knowledge and skills of the MTLE training program, we can significantly help reduce the number of traumatic injuries and devastating loss of life. Law enforcement officers dedicate their careers and lives to protect the public and greater good, and the MTLE training program is dedicated to helping officers *survive and prevail* in the line of duty.

APPENDIX A

SUMMARY OF CORE MEDICAL TACTICS FOR LAW ENFORCEMENT TRAINING CONCEPTS

Medical Tactics for Law Enforcement (MTLE) four core training concepts

1. *Mindset:* Conditioning the mind to help limit the negative effects of extreme stress and improve critical decision making in life-threatening situations.
2. *Mechanics:* Understanding the fundamentals of penetrating trauma and separating medical fact from fiction.
3. *Management:* Recognizing and learning when to treat life-threatening injuries.
4. *Movement.* Safely and effectively planning and performing assists, carries, and drags to make it out of the hot zone alive.

Our own worst enemy, the natural human stress response (as explained relative to the first core training concept *mindset*):

1. *Perception:* An individual's interpretation and expectation of unfolding events, which are dependent on a conceptual or actual frame of reference.
2. *Fear:* An individual's learned response, which is frequently inaccurate or inappropriate.
3. *Mindset:* An individual's psychological preparedness, which responds to the fear.
4. *Physiology:* An individual's innate survival countermeasures, including respiration and heart rate, which are designed to maximize the body's physical performance in the face of danger or perceived fear and the need to fight or run.
5. *Response:* The sequential interplay of perception, fear, mindset, and physiological components, which culminate in leading an individual to make a decision and take action!

APPENDIX B

SUMMARY OF MEDICAL TACTICS FOR LAW ENFORCEMENT

Life-Saving Script At-a-Glance and Detail

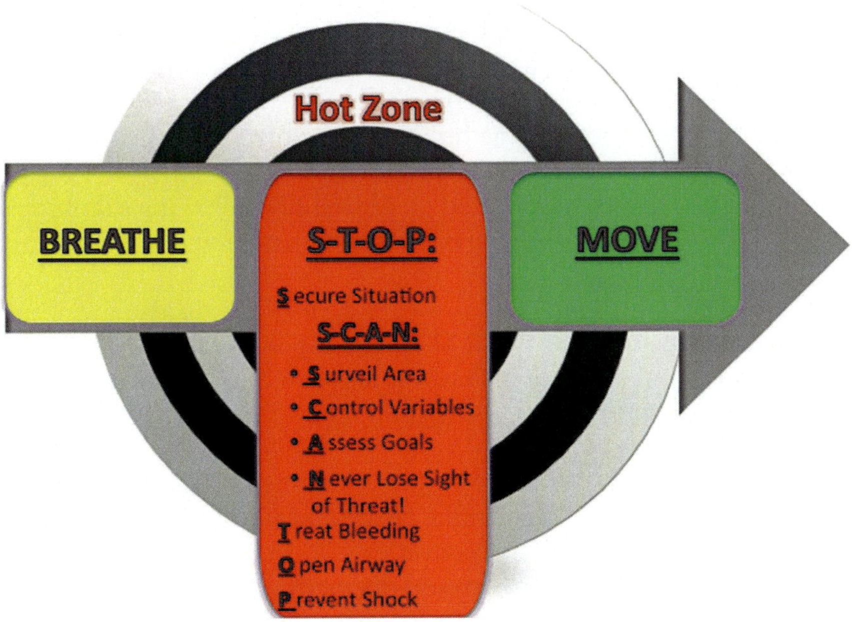

Detail:

1. **BREATHE**
   - 1.1. *Take critical timeout before taking action to just breathe:*
     - 1.1.1. Increase oxygenation of body's circulatory system
     - 1.1.2. Calm heart rate and blood pressure
     - 1.1.3. Curb fear and anxiety
     - 1.1.4. Compose self and gain control over mind and body
     - 1.1.5. Improve ability to maintain tactical mindset and function under stress
     - 1.1.6. Prioritize actions
   - 1.2. *Perform tactical dynamic breathing technique:*
     - 1.2.1. Rest tongue against roof of mouth
     - 1.2.2. Inhale through nose, consciously moving diaphragm, or belly, muscle located between chest and abdomen downward and outward to inflate lungs
     - 1.2.3. In performing this type of breathing, as you breathe in and hold your breath, you also bear down through your chest and abdomen as if you were going to perform a bowel movement. Bearing down this way actually helps to dramatically reduce your heart rate. Then you release the hold and forcibly exhale the air
     - 1.2.4. Release the hold and forcibly exhale air from lungs through puckered or pursed lips, allowing diaphragm muscle to move back inward and upward to neutral position
2. **S-T-O-P**
   (S-ecure the situation, T-reat bleeding, O-pen airway, P-revent shock)
   - 2.1. **S-ecure the situation:** Perform a **S-C-A-N** (**S**-urveil area, **C**-ontrol variables, **A**-sess goals, **N**-ever lose sight of the threat!)
     - 2.1.1. *S-urveil area:*
       - 2.1.1.1. Identify injured victims and possible threats
       - 2.1.1.2. Determine need to perform victim rescues or body recoveries
       - 2.1.1.3. Perform remote victim assessment:
         - 2.1.1.3.1. Confirm *injured victim's breathing airway is not obstructed:* Ability to respond verbally; if unable to respond verbally, observe for rise and fall of chest to confirm breathing
         - 2.1.1.3.2. Assess victim for shock: Ability to respond verbally and make logical

sense; visible injuries and disabilities; or uncontrollable, spontaneous movements of body

- 2.1.2. *C-ontrol variables:*
  - 2.1.2.1. Determine variables within versus beyond control
  - 2.1.2.2. Consider how to minimize risks to self and others at scene
- 2.1.3. *A-ssess goals:* Devise plan to survive and prevail based on control variables, focusing on two key goals:
  - 2.1.3.1. Taking cover to conceal self and others from offender
  - 2.1.3.2. Extracting self and victims from hot zone to safety:
    - 2.1.3.2.1. Consider vulnerable points along rescue route
    - 2.1.3.2.2. Consider needs to assist, carry or drag victims along route to safety plus distance and travel time
- 2.1.4. *N-ever lose sight of the threat!*
  - 2.1.4.1. Apply strategic survival tactics to eliminate, or at least minimize, exposure to threat first before treating injuries
  - 2.1.4.2. Prepare to adapt response to different situations!

2.2. **Treat bleeding:**

- 2.2.1. *Focus on two key goals:*
  - 2.2.1.1. Prevent further blood loss
  - 2.2.1.2. Restore downstream blood flow
- 2.2.2. *Remember what is realistic to treat in the street:* Bleeding from head, arms, and legs
  - 2.2.2.1. Bleeding from abdomen and chest is typically more difficult to treat
  - 2.2.2.2. For more serious, untreatable bleeding, plan expedited extraction of victim for immediate transport to trauma center
- 2.2.3. *Confirm downstream blood flow in injured victim:*
  - 2.2.3.1. Check peripheral pulse on underside of wrist
  - 2.2.3.2. Check efficiency of capillary refilling, pressing firmly on fingernail, releasing finger and counting seconds for return of normal tissue color

- 2.2.4. *Prepare to treat bleeding and protect self:* Put on protective medical gloves first!
- 2.2.5. *Use the Trauma Rapid Intervention Kit (TRIK):* Contains all tools used in MTLE training class to treat bleeding
- 2.2.6. *If you are caught in a situation without a TRIK:* Improvise!
  - 2.2.6.1. Use best available material on hand to make wound dressing
  - 2.2.6.2. Carry a knife, and the world is your bandage!
- 2.2.7. *Apply principles of pressure to control bleeding based on location of injury, amount of bleeding, and environment:*
  - 2.2.7.1. Principles of Pressure I: Apply direct pressure to wound
  - 2.2.7.2. Principles of Pressure II: Apply direct pressure where needed with packing into the wound and a pressure dressing
  - 2.2.7.3. Principles of Pressure III: Apply packing and firm pressure or, if necessary, a tourniquet upstream of wound
  - 2.2.7.4. Principles of Pressure IV: Apply hemostatic, or blood-clotting agent, with packing material, direct pressure and, preferably, a pressure dressing

2.3. **Open airway:**

- 2.3.1. *Assess injured victim's ability to verbally respond* (if you are injured but able to speak, then vocalize to your partner and fellow officers your condition, if possible)
- 2.3.2. *If victim is marginally or completely verbally unresponsive (semiconscious or unconscious) but still breathing:* Consider using a nasal pharyngeal airway to stabilize breathing ability
- 2.3.3. *If victim is both unresponsive and no longer breathing upon closer examination:* Discontinue rescue efforts
- 2.3.4. *Treat ALL penetrating chest wounds as open pneumothoraxes, "sucking chest wounds:"*
  - 2.3.4.1. Apply pressure/release dressing over hole in victim's chest
  - 2.3.4.2. Seal down *three* of four sides of dressing with medical tape (leave *fourth* side unsealed)

2.4. **Prevent shock:**
 2.4.1. *ALWAYS assume risk for shock: Victim may present as conscious, semiconscious, or unconscious; and pale, sweaty, shivering, confused, agitated, or scared*
 2.4.2. *Secure weapons—yours and his—to prevent a confused, agitated or scared victim from grabbing them*
 2.4.3. *Assess seriousness of a victim's shock potential:*
  2.4.3.1. Assess victim's level of consciousness (ability to respond verbally and make logical sense)
  2.4.3.2. Assess blood loss: (> three liters or approx. three-foot diameter pool = severe shock, requiring blood transfusion; > 5 liters or approx. 4-foot pool of blood = game over)
  2.4.3.3. Check for blood-soaked stains on clothing (harder to see on darker clothing)
  2.4.3.4. Use trauma shears to expose injuries to more accurately assess degree of blood loss
 2.4.4. *ALWAYS treat for shock, regardless of type of injury and degree of blood loss:*
  2.4.4.1. Elevate legs to improve upstream blood flow to heart and brain (remember "face pale, raise tale")
  2.4.4.2. Wrap victim with blanket, jacket, or other material to provide warmth and prevent hypothermia (wrap victim's head and torso first then rest of body)
  2.4.4.3. Consider options for immediate evacuation of victim in critical condition to nearest trauma center for treatment

3. **MOVE**
 3.1. *Confirm ability to move, performing quick self-test (applies to injured victims as well):*
  3.1.1. Try to move body from head to toe to test major physical and fine motor skill functions
  3.1.2. Look about in multiple directions
  3.1.3. Identify any injuries and limitations to movement
  3.1.4. Assess whether assisted extraction is needed
 3.2. *Stage 1: Move from hot zone to safer zone:*
  3.2.1. *Consider situational variables:* Type and degree of injuries sustained, number of officers available to help,

escape route terrain and distance, and need to defend against any remaining threats

3.2.2. *Choose among extraction method options based on situational variables:*

3.2.2.1. Assist: One- or two-man, high-shoulder assist

3.2.2.2. Drag: One- or two-man drag

3.2.2.3. Carry: One-man, fireman's carry (generally, NOT recommended); two-man, forward-facing carry; three- or four-man superman carry; or other improvised carry (such as a wheelchair, cart, or rug)

3.2.3. *Exercise creativity and resourcefulness:* Utilize whatever objects are available to facilitate rescue effort

3.3. *Stage 2: Transport to nearest trauma center for comprehensive emergency care:*

3.3.1. *Consider transport mode options:*

3.3.1.1. Ambulance (generally most preferable, although exceptions may apply depending on situational factors and urgency)

3.3.1.2. Squad car

3.3.1.3. Other improvised modes, such as civilian vehicle

3.3.2. *Load victim into transport vehicle:*

3.3.2.1. Simultaneously manage victim's airway and other injuries

3.3.2.2. Use victim's weight when loading into vehicle

3.3.2.3. If there is room in vehicle and help available, position one or two rescuers inside backseat or back hatch area to receive victim

APPENDIX C

SUMMARY OF TRAUMA RAPID INTERVENTION KIT: SEVEN ESSENTIAL LIFE-SAVING TOOLS AND KEY DESIGN FEATURES

Seven Essential Life-Saving Tools

The Trauma Rapid Intervention Kit (TRIK) contains all of the tools used in the Medical Tactics for Law Enforcement training class:

1. *Large nitrile exam gloves (2 pairs):* The gloves are lightweight, durable, and latex-free. They may protect either one or two rescuers from direct contact with blood or other bodily fluids.
2. *PVC sterile nasopharyngeal airway, also known as an NPA, and lubricant:* Designed for airway management of the responsive or unresponsive patient. The non-toxic, water-based lubricant allows the NPA to slide through the patient's nose and past his soft palate, keeping the airway open and secure.
3. *Trauma shears* (7″): The jaws of these shears are sturdy enough to cut through automobile seatbelts, denim, and leather, while the blunted tip and angled action help prevent undue harm of the injured victim.
4. *Medical tape* (1″ × 30′): The roll of tape comes pre-started for those instances in which adrenaline has blunted the body's fine motor skills. The adhesive is hypoallergenic and will not painfully adhere to skin. Useful in potentially any and every medical emergency.
5. *Emergency bandage, also known as Israeli bandage* (4″): This versatile and indispensable bandage tool for hemorrhage, or bleeding,

Trauma Rapid Intervention Kit (TRIK) Components.

control has both compression and tourniquet functions. The bandage may be applied effectively almost anywhere on the body to manage severe bleeding. Additionally, the bandage may be modified for use as a sling in supporting an injured limb.

6. *Abdominal bandage, also known as an ABD pad* (15″ × 9″): The sterile gauze ABD pad is bulky enough to pack into a large wound to help control bleeding and wide enough to cover and protect a burn. Used with the shears and tape, the ABD pad can be customized to control a variety of bleeds.
7. *Mylar emergency blanket* (84″ × 52″): This highly insulating, weatherproof blanket is coated to reflect the patient's body heat back upon himself, protecting him against hypothermia and shock, both of which are potentially fatal conditions.

Key design features:

- Comprehensive, yet lightweight and easy to carry and use
- Practical and highly versatile application for various key trauma care concepts
- Compact and small enough to fit in the cargo pocket of any battle dress uniform or duty pant, external tactical vest carrier pocket, or modular, lightweight, load-carrying equipment pouch
- Vacuum sealed packaging is weatherproof and tamper-proof—it even floats!
- "Member Tested, Member Approved" seal from the National Tactical Officers Association

INDEX

M

N

O

P

R

S

SOURCES

ARTICLES

Ander, R., Cook, P. J., Ludwig, J., and Pollack, H. "The University of Chicago Crime Lab: Gun Violence Among School-Age Youth in Chicago." *The University of Chicago Crime Lab* (March 2009): 13. http://crimelab.uchicago.edu/gun_violence/report.shtml.

Aveni, Thomas J. "Officer-Involved Shootings: What We Didn't Know Has Hurt Us." *The Police Policy Studies Council* (2002).

Baker, A. "A Hail of Bullets, a Heap of Uncertainty," *New York Times* (December 9, 2007). http://www.nytimes.com/2007/12/09/weekinreview/09baker.html?pagewanted=all&_r=0

Bascom, Nick. "Brainy ballplayers, Elite athletes get their heads in the game." *ScienceNews* 14 (January 2012): 22–25. http://www.sciencenews.org/.

Centerwall, Brandon S. "Television and Violence: The Scale of the Problem and Where to Go From Here," *Journal of the American Medical Association* 267(22) (June 1992):3059–63. http://jama.jamanetwork.com/article.aspx?articleid=397737.

Cornwell, E. E., III, Belzberg, H., Hennigan, K., Maxson, C., Montoya, G., Rosenbluth, A., Velmahos, G. C., Berne, T. C., and Demetriades, D. "Emergency Medical Services (EMS) vs Non-EMS Transport of Critically Injured Patients, a Prospective Evaluation." *Archives of Surgery, The JAMA Network* 135(3) (200):315–319, 1–8. http://archsurg.jamanetwork.com/journal.aspx.

Dennis, A., and Bir, C. Unpublished research data. 2012.

Dorlac, W. C., DeBakey, M. E., Holcomb, J. B., Fagan, S. P., Kwong, K. L., Dorlac, G. R., Schreiber, M. A., Persse, D. E., Moore, F. A., and Mattox, K. L. "Mortality from Isolated Civilian Penetrating Extremity Injury." *The Journal of TRAUMA® Injury, Infection and Critical Care,* 59 (July 2005) 1: 217–222.

Dunham, Will. David Storey, ed. "Disco tune 'Stayin' Alive' could save your life," *Reuters,* 16 (October 2008). http://www.reuters.com/article/2008/10/16/us-heart-beegees-idUSTRE49F86520081016.

Federal Bureau of Investigation. "Killed in the Line of Duty: A study of Selected Felonious Killings of Law Enforcement Officers: Conducted by Uniform Crime Reports Section," Federal Bureau of Investigation, United States Department of Justice. Washington, D.C.: Federal Bureau of Investigation. 1992.

Hurley, Michael J., Deputy Inspector, Commanding Officer. "2006 Firearms Discharge Report." Police Academy Firearms and Tactics Section, New York City Police Department. www.nyclu.org/files/nypd_firearms_report_102207.pdf.

Kelly, Raymond W., Farrell, Michael J., and Gerrish, John P. "Annual Firearms Discharge Report 2007," Office of Management Analysis and Planning, New York City Police Department. www.nyc.gov/html/nypd/.../2007_firearms_discharge_report.pdf.

Reilly, B., Evans, A., Schaider, J., Das, K., Calvin, J., Moran, L., Roberts, R., and Martinez, E., "Impact of a Clinical Decision Rule on Hospital Triage of Patients with Suspected Acute Cardiac Ischemia in the Emergency Department." *JAMA* 288 no.3 (July 17, 2002): 342–350.

Smith-Bindman, R., Lipson, J., Marcus, R., Kim, K. P., Mahesh, M., Gould, R., Berrington de González, A., and Miglioretti, D. L. "Radiation Dose Associated with Common Computed Tomography Examinations and the Associated Lifetime Attributable Risk of Cancer," *Archives of Internal Medicine* 169(22) (December 14, 2009): 2078–86. doi: 10.1001/archinternmed.2009.427.

Sztajnkrycer, Matthew D., Lewinski, Bill, and Buhrmaster, Scott, "Leave No One Behind: Downed-Officer Rescue and Risk Perception." *FBI Law Enforcement Bulletin, Research Forum* (May 2010). http://www.fbi.gov/stats-services/publications/law-enforcement-bulletin/May-2010/research-forum.

Vonk, Kathleen D. "Police Performance Under Stress." *Law & Order* 56, 10 (2008): 1–13. www.loukatactical.com/articles/Heart_Rate_and_Performance_Under_Stress_Article_to.pdf.

Wald, Matthew L. "Plane Crew Is Credited for Nimble Reaction." *The New York Times* (16 January 2009). http://www.nytimes.com/2009/01/16/nyregion/16pilot.html?_r=1.

Wound Data and Munitions Effectiveness Team. *The WDMET Study, Wound Data and Munitions Effectiveness Team* (1970). Original data in possession of Uniformed Services University of the Health Sciences, Bethesda, MD.

Books:

Asken, Michael J. *MindSighting: Mental Toughness Skills for Police Officers in High Stress Situations.* Camp Hill, Pa: Mindsighting, 2008.

Asken, Michael J., Grossman, Dave, and Christensen, Loren, W. *Warrior Mindset,* 1st Ed. Millstadt, IL: Human Factor Research Group. 2010.

Forgey, W. W. and Wilderness Medical Society. *Wilderness Medical Society Practice Guidelines for Wilderness Emergency Care,* 5th Ed. Guilford, CT: FalconGuides. 2006.

Gladwell, Malcolm. *Blink: The Power of Thinking Without Thinking* 1st Ed. New York: Little, Brown and Company. 2005. http://www.gladwell.com/blink/index.html.

Grossman, Dave and Christensen, Loren W. *On Combat, The Psychology and Physiology of Deadly Conflict in War and Peace,* 3rd Ed. Millstadt, IL: Warrior Science Publications. 2008.

Klinger, David. *Into the Kill Zone: A Cop's Eye View of Deadly Force.* San Francisco: Jossey-Bass. 2006.

Seligman, Martin E. P., *Helplessness: On Depression, Development, and Death.* San Francisco: W. H. Freeman. 1975. ISBN 0–7167–0752–7; paperback reprint edition, W. H. Freeman, 1992, ISBN 0–7167–2328-X.

Siddle, B. K. *Sharpening the Warriors Edge: The Psychology & Science of Training.* Millstadt, IL: Human Factor Research Group. 2005. Cited in Kathleen D. Vonk, Police Performance under Stress, *Law & Order,* Vol. 56, No. 10 2008.

PRESENTATION

Butler, Frank. "Tactical Combat Casualty Care Defense Health Board Update." Presentation (9 March 2009):9–10. www.health.mil/dhb/downloads/Butler%20TCCC

PRESS RELEASE

Lloyd, J. "Pop Song 'Stayin' Alive' Helps People Perform Chest Compressions For CPR." *American College of Emergency Physicians,* press release (27 October, 2008). http://www.acep.org/content.aspx?id=45601

WEBSITE

Federal Bureau of Investigation, U.S. Department of Justice. "Law Enforcement Officers Killed and Assaulted, 2008." (October 2009). http://www2.fbi.gov/ucr/killed/2008/

Federal Bureau of Investigation, U.S. Department of Justice. "Law Enforcement Officers Killed and Assaulted, 2011." (November 2012). http://www.fbi.gov/about-us/cjis/ucr/leoka/2011/leoka-home

PHOTOS

Iwanicki, Michael, D.O., Director of Trauma Services, Co-Director of Critical Care Services, Advocate Good Samaritan Hospital, Downers Grove, Illinois.

VIDEOS

Cops, Video #546. 20th Century Fox, 2003.

History Channel. *Shootout!: North Hollywood Shootout.* Feb 28, 1997. Hollywood: History Channel, 2005. Video, 50 minutes. http://shop.history.com/shootout-north-hollywood-shootout-dvd/detail.php?p=69246